AngularJS Directives Cookbook

Extend the capabilities of AngularJS and build dynamic web applications by creating customized directives with a collection of more than 30 recipes

Fernando Monteiro

BIRMINGHAM - MUMBAI

AngularJS Directives Cookbook

Copyright © 2015 Packt Publishing

All rights reserved. No part of this book may be reproduced, stored in a retrieval system, or transmitted in any form or by any means, without the prior written permission of the publisher, except in the case of brief quotations embedded in critical articles or reviews.

Every effort has been made in the preparation of this book to ensure the accuracy of the information presented. However, the information contained in this book is sold without warranty, either express or implied. Neither the author, nor Packt Publishing, and its dealers and distributors will be held liable for any damages caused or alleged to be caused directly or indirectly by this book.

Packt Publishing has endeavored to provide trademark information about all of the companies and products mentioned in this book by the appropriate use of capitals. However, Packt Publishing cannot guarantee the accuracy of this information.

First published: November 2015

Production reference: 1261115

Published by Packt Publishing Ltd.
Livery Place
35 Livery Street
Birmingham B3 2PB, UK.

ISBN 978-1-78439-589-6

www.packtpub.com

Credits

Author
Fernando Monteiro

Reviewers
Mark Coleman
Patrick Gillespie
Aakash Patel
Adam Štipák

Commissioning Editor
Ashwin Nair

Acquisition Editor
Tushar Gupta

Content Development Editor
Pooja Mhapsekar

Technical Editor
Vivek Arora

Copy Editor
Roshni Banerjee

Project Coordinator
Shipra Chawhan

Proofreader
Safis Editing

Indexer
Rekha Nair

Production Coordinator
Aparna Bhagat

Cover Work
Aparna Bhagat

About the Author

Fernando Monteiro is a frontend engineer, speaker, open source contributor, and the mind behind the Responsive Boilerplate—a CSS library built with Less.js for responsive layouts. He contributes several articles and materials on design, development, and user experience on his blog and for the entire web community.

He is passionate about web standards, frontend development, JavaScript, and mobile design, and he spent the last 13 years creating high-end graphic and web experiences. He has also authored two books, namely, *Instant HTML5 Responsive Table Design How-to* and *Learning Single-page Web Application Development*, both by Packt Publishing.

Currently, he works full-time with AngularJS as a frontend engineer in one of the most important genetic analysis companies in Brazil. You can find more about him at www.newaeonweb.com.br.

> I would like to thank everyone who supported me on this journey, my son, Mateus, for always being by my side; Ellen for all the moments of encouragement; Henrique; my mother, Paschoalina Patrizzi; and my sister, Marcia Monteiro.
>
> I would also like to thank all the staff at Packt Publishing, who I was directly in contact with, for their patience and support.

About the Reviewers

Mark Coleman is a full stack developer focusing on the latest in web technologies. Mark enjoys learning about new programming trends. Mark also likes to share his knowledge by attending local development groups and blogging (`kramnameloc.com`) about programming topics. When Mark is not absorbing everything development, he enjoys photography, anything pertaining to The Simpsons, and is a part-time craft beer/bacon aficionado.

Patrick Gillespie is a senior software engineer at Proteus Technologies. He has both a bachelor's and a master's degree in computer science. In his spare time, he enjoys photography, spending time with his family, and working on web projects for his personal site (`patorjk.com`).

Aakash Patel is the cofounder of Flytenow, which provides a way to share rides in small planes. He writes AngularJS and develops web applications.

Adam Štipák is currently a full stack developer. He has more than 9 years of professional experience with web development. He likes technologies pertaining to web development, including frontend, backend, and so on. He likes open source in general.

Adam works for diagnose.me as the head of development. He worked at Sygic prior to that as a backend developer and scrum master.

You can find him at `http://newpope.org`.

www.PacktPub.com

Support files, eBooks, discount offers, and more

For support files and downloads related to your book, please visit www.PacktPub.com.

Did you know that Packt offers eBook versions of every book published, with PDF and ePub files available? You can upgrade to the eBook version at www.PacktPub.com and as a print book customer, you are entitled to a discount on the eBook copy. Get in touch with us at service@packtpub.com for more details.

At www.PacktPub.com, you can also read a collection of free technical articles, sign up for a range of free newsletters and receive exclusive discounts and offers on Packt books and eBooks.

https://www2.packtpub.com/books/subscription/packtlib

Do you need instant solutions to your IT questions? PacktLib is Packt's online digital book library. Here, you can search, access, and read Packt's entire library of books.

Why Subscribe?

- Fully searchable across every book published by Packt
- Copy and paste, print, and bookmark content
- On demand and accessible via a web browser

Free Access for Packt account holders

If you have an account with Packt at www.PacktPub.com, you can use this to access PacktLib today and view 9 entirely free books. Simply use your login credentials for immediate access.

Table of Contents

Preface	**iii**
Chapter 1: Dealing with Modal and Tabs Directives	**1**
Introduction	1
Using inline HTML templates	2
Creating a simple modal directive	4
Loading external templates for best practices	7
Using the link function	11
Dealing with tabs without Bootstrap UI directives	13
Chapter 2: Building a Navbar Custom Directive	**23**
Introduction	23
Building a navbar directive	24
Directory structure for common components	29
Directive's controller function	32
Using the data attribute to HTML5 compile	35
Chapter 3: Customizing and Using Bootstrap UI Directives	**39**
Introduction	39
Dealing with modal directives	40
Creating tab directives	46
The isolate $scope	52
Building accordion tab directives	56
Loading dynamic content	60
Chapter 4: Creating Interactive jQuery UI Directives	**63**
Introduction	63
A simple directive example	64
Manipulating the DOM with jQuery	66
The compile and link functions	68

Table of Contents

    Creating the jQuery UI draggable directive   **71**
    Creating the jQuery UI droppable directive   **73**

Chapter 5: Implementing Custom Directives with Yeoman Generators   77
    Introduction   77
    Creating the baseline app with generator-angm   78
    Generator best practices   80
    How to implement the ngMap directive   82
    Using the Angular-Loading-Bar directive   85
    Implementing the ng-grid directive   88

Chapter 6: Using Directives to Develop Interface Components   95
    Introduction   95
    Creating an Off Canvas menu   95
    Applying custom CSS   103
    Building a shopping cart   106

Chapter 7: Building Directives with Dynamic Templates   117
    Introduction   117
    Using dynamic templates on directives   118
    The compile function   125
    Organizing dynamic directives on shared folders   126
    Mixing different content on templates   128

Chapter 8: Creating Reusable Directives   137
    Introduction   137
    How to scale an AngularJS project to use reusable directives   138
    Building a directive as an interface component   145
    Creating a form directive with custom validation   157

Chapter 9: Directive Unit Testing with Karma and Jasmine   165
    Introduction   165
    How to test AngularJS apps using Karma and Karma Runner   166
    Writing tests for directives with Jasmine   173
    Testing elements when the scope changes   180

Index   185

Preface

Directives make up an important part of AngularJS development to manipulate the Document Object Model (DOM), route events to event handler functions, and much more. Through the use of custom directives, we can build applications with a rich user interface. Although the built-in directives such as ng-repeat, ng-show, and ng-hide cover many different scenarios, you will often need to create specific directives for your application. This book will give you an overview of how to create and customize AngularJS directives, with best practices in mind.

What this book covers

Throughout this book, we'll explore different ways to build AngularJS directives and understand all the elements that make up a directive.

We will cover fundamental concepts about scope, link, $compile, external templates, reusable components, and Directives Unit Testing.

Mastering how to create and customize AngularJS directives, by the end of this book you will be able to work comfortably with modular AngularJS applications using custom directives to create rich web interface components.

Although some points are advanced, you'll be prepared to understand the core concepts and how to choose or create the right directive for your project.

Chapter 1, *Dealing with Modal and Tabs Directives*, presents some alternatives to create simple interface components such as Modal and tabs using tips and exploring best practices to cover the most important points of creating and dealing with directives.

Chapter 2, *Building a Navbar Custom Directive*, focuses on building a custom navbar with menu links as a directive component. You will learn how to manipulate the DOM to show and hide user information using these custom directives and how to structure an AngularJS application to use shared components.

Preface

Chapter 3, *Customizing and Using Bootstrap UI Directives*, throws light on Bootstrap UI directives and explains how to extend and customize some components, exploring external templates and custom CSS customization, showing some component examples in real-case scenarios.

Chapter 4, *Creating Interactive jQuery UI Directives*, explains how to use jQuery and the jQuery UI to build some interface components with a comprehensive approach to how jQuery manipulates the DOM in AngularJS applications using IDs and selectors.

Chapter 5, *Implementing Custom Directives with Yeoman Generators*, shows how to use a Yeoman generator to create custom directives of ongoing projects, how to implement some useful directives, such as ngMap, and more.

Chapter 6, *Using Directives to Develop Interface Components*, demonstrates how to build a micro e-commerce application combining different types of custom directives.

Chapter 7, *Building Directives with Dynamic Templates*, explains how to build directives to use and load dynamic templates, provides a comparison of inline templates and external templates, explains more about the Compile function, and shows how to organize custom directives on shared folders.

Chapter 8, *Creating Reusable Directives*, shows how we can organize an AngularJS application and prepare it to be scalable with the use of shared directives, how to build chart directives, and explores some points about naming conventions, code organization, and best practices.

Chapter 9, *Directive Unit Testing with Karma and Jasmine*, covers how to configure and use Karma and Karma Runner to test custom directives using the Jasmine framework and explains how to deal with scope change and testing elements.

What you need for this book

All the examples in this book use open source solutions and can be downloaded for free from the links provided in each chapter.

We use AngularJS and a Yeoman Generator to build all the examples. You can find the link to each tool in every chapter, mainly in the *Getting ready* section.

Also, you will need Node.js installed on your machine and tools such as Grunt, Yeoman, and Bower.

You can find how to install these tools using the following links:

- Node.js: `https://nodejs.org/en/`
- Grunt.js: `http://gruntjs.com/`
- Bower: `http://bower.io/`
- Yeoman: `http://yeoman.io/`

Preface

You can use the text editor of your choice, but in *Chapter 9, Directive Unit Testing with Karma and Jasmine*, we strongly recommend the use of WebStorm. However, the tasks can be accomplished with a simple editor.

You can download a trial version from WebStorm at `https://www.jetbrains.com/webstorm/`.

A modern browser will be very helpful too. We use Chrome, but feel free to use your preferred one. We recommend the latest versions of Safari, Firefox, Chrome, IE, or Opera.

Also, if you need some help with the markup, you can download the code examples.

Who this book is for

This book is meant for developers with AngularJS experience who want to extend their knowledge of how to create or customize directives in any type of AngularJS application. Some knowledge of modern tools such as Yeoman and Bower will be quite useful, but is not mandatory.

Sections

In this book, you will find several headings that appear frequently (Getting ready, How to do it, How it works, There's more, and See also).

To give clear instructions on how to complete a recipe, we use these sections as follows:

Getting ready

This section tells you what to expect in the recipe, and describes how to set up any software or any preliminary settings required for the recipe.

How to do it...

This section contains the steps required to follow the recipe.

How it works...

This section usually consists of a detailed explanation of what happened in the previous section.

There's more...

This section consists of additional information about the recipe in order to make the reader more knowledgeable about the recipe.

Preface

See also

This section provides helpful links to other useful information for the recipe.

Conventions

In this book, you will find a number of text styles that distinguish between different kinds of information. Here are some examples of these styles and an explanation of their meaning.

Code words in text, database table names, folder names, filenames, file extensions, pathnames, dummy URLs, user input, and Twitter handles are shown as follows: "We will use a simple HTML file with AngularJS script in the `head` tag."

A block of code is set as follows:

```
<script type="text/ng-template" id="first.html">
  <div class="tab-content" id="1">
    <h1>First Tab</h1>
    <p>Simple tab 1</p>
  </div>
</script>
```

Any command-line input or output is written as follows:

`npm install generator-angm -g`

New terms and **important words** are shown in bold. Words that you see on the screen, for example, in menus or dialog boxes, appear in the text like this: "When we click on the **Add to Cart** button, the directive shows a simple message."

Warnings or important notes appear in a box like this.

Tips and tricks appear like this.

Reader feedback

Feedback from our readers is always welcome. Let us know what you think about this book—what you liked or disliked. Reader feedback is important for us as it helps us develop titles that you will really get the most out of.

To send us general feedback, simply e-mail `feedback@packtpub.com`, and mention the book's title in the subject of your message.

If there is a topic that you have expertise in and you are interested in either writing or contributing to a book, see our author guide at `www.packtpub.com/authors`.

Customer support

Now that you are the proud owner of a Packt book, we have a number of things to help you to get the most from your purchase.

Downloading the example code

You can download the example code files from your account at `http://www.packtpub.com` for all the Packt Publishing books you have purchased. If you purchased this book elsewhere, you can visit `http://www.packtpub.com/support` and register to have the files e-mailed directly to you.

Errata

Although we have taken every care to ensure the accuracy of our content, mistakes do happen. If you find a mistake in one of our books—maybe a mistake in the text or the code—we would be grateful if you could report this to us. By doing so, you can save other readers from frustration and help us improve subsequent versions of this book. If you find any errata, please report them by visiting `http://www.packtpub.com/submit-errata`, selecting your book, clicking on the **Errata Submission Form** link, and entering the details of your errata. Once your errata are verified, your submission will be accepted and the errata will be uploaded to our website or added to any list of existing errata under the Errata section of that title.

To view the previously submitted errata, go to `https://www.packtpub.com/books/content/support` and enter the name of the book in the search field. The required information will appear under the **Errata** section.

Preface

Piracy

Piracy of copyrighted material on the Internet is an ongoing problem across all media. At Packt, we take the protection of our copyright and licenses very seriously. If you come across any illegal copies of our works in any form on the Internet, please provide us with the location address or website name immediately so that we can pursue a remedy.

Please contact us at `copyright@packtpub.com` with a link to the suspected pirated material.

We appreciate your help in protecting our authors and our ability to bring you valuable content.

Questions

If you have a problem with any aspect of this book, you can contact us at `questions@packtpub.com`, and we will do our best to address the problem.

1
Dealing with Modal and Tabs Directives

In this chapter, we will cover:

- Using inline HTML templates
- Creating a simple modal directive
- Loading external templates for best practices
- Using the link function
- Dealing with tabs without Bootstrap UI directives

Introduction

Directives make up an important part in AngularJS applications with AngularJS. They manipulate the **Document Object Model** (**DOM**), route events to event handler functions, and much more. Through the use of custom directives, we can build applications with a rich user interface.

Although the built-in directives such as `ng-repeat`, `ng-show`, and `ng-hide` cover many different scenarios, you will often need to create application-specific directives. This chapter will give you an overview on how to create and customize simple AngularJS directives, with the best practices in mind.

We assume that you already know what directives are, so let's check how to create and customize some simple directives to manipulate the DOM.

Using inline HTML templates

The basic form to create an AngularJS directive is very simple and intuitive. Let's take a look at a basic way to declare a directive using inline HTML:

```
.directive("directiveName",function () {

  return {
    restrict: 'A',

    controller: function() {
      // Directive Controller
    },

    link: function() {
      // Link function
    },
    template: ''
  }
});
```

As the name implies, we include the HTML template within the code of the directive through the `template` property.

Let's see a practical example to show some text on the screen.

Getting ready

The following example is very simple and easy to understand. Imagine that we have set up an AngularJS application called `app` and want to display some simple text in the browser with the following content: `Hello Simple Directive`.

For this recipe, we will use a simple HTML file with AngularJS script in the `head` tag.

Add `myFirstDirective` as a dependence to the `app` application:

```
angular.module('app', ['myFirstDirectives']);
```

How to do it...

So, we can declare and inject the module that contains our directive into our application. Following the best practices to include new dependencies on the AngularJS application, we called the directive as `helloSimpleDirective`:

```
angular.module('myFirstDirective')

.directive('helloSimpleDirective', function() {
 return {
    scope: true,   // inherits child scope from parent.
    restrict: 'E', // An Element Directive.
    replace: true,
    template: '<h3>Hello Simple Directive</h3>'
  };
});
```

 Note that we have declared here as an element directive.

How it works...

Now, before we look into the code, we need to remember that we have the following four types of directives and that we can use more than one each time:

- An HTML element (`<directive-type></directive-type>`), represented by the letter E
- An attribute on an element (`<input type="text" directive-type/>`), represented by the letter A
- As a class (`<input type="text" class="directive-type"/>`), represented by the letter C
- As a comment (`<!--directive:directive-type-->`), represented by the letter M

We will see more about this in the later chapters.

In the first line of code, we named the application module as `myFirstDirective` and added the directive called `helloSimpleDirective` as a module. It's very simple to use this directive too. Just declare it like any other HTML tag (in this case, an element), as shown in the following code:

```
<hello-simple-directive></hello-simple-directive>
```

Dealing with Modal and Tabs Directives

In the previous code, our `angular.module('app', [myFirstDirective])` function serves to register the new directive to the AngularJS application. On the directive, the first string argument is the directive name `'hellosimpledirective'` and the second argument is a function that returns a **Directive Definition Object (DDO)**. Also, if the directive has some external object/service dependencies such as `$http`, `$resource`, and `$compile`, among others, they can be injected here.

Note that we have declared the directive as an HTML element, and the sign - has delimited strings to camelCase, so the name `helloSimpleDirective` will be converted to `hello-simple-directive` to be used as the directive name.

In this basic example, we just print on the screen the h3 HTML `tag` with the text `Hello Simple Directive`.

See also

- You can read more about directives on the official AngularJS documentation at https://docs.angularjs.org/guide/directive

Creating a simple modal directive

Modal windows are interface components often used in web applications. Building them is very simple and is done using libraries such as Dojo or jQuery, but implementing them in AngularJS applications is not as simple, since the DOM manipulation is restricted to directives.

Next, we will see how to use this component in a very simple way.

Getting ready

Let's start placing the following HTML code in a new blank page. The following code has all the basic requisites to illustrate the example:

```html
<!DOCTYPE html>
<html>
<head>
<script src="https://ajax.googleapis.com/ajax/libs/angularjs/1.3.x/angular.js"></script>
<title>Modal Window Directive</title>
<style>
  .modal-overlay {
  position:absolute;
  z-index:9999;
  top:0;
```

```css
    left:0;
    width:100%;
    height:100%;
    background-color:#000;
    opacity: 0.8;
}
.modal-background {
    z-index:10000;
    position: absolute;
    top: 50%;
    left: 50%;
    transform: translate(-50%, -50%);
    background-color: #fff;

}
.modal-content {
    padding:10px;
    text-align: center;
}
.modal-close {
    position: absolute;
    top: 5px;
    right: 5px;
    padding: 5px;
    cursor: pointer;
    display: inline-block;
}
</style>
</head>
<body ng-app='SimpleModal'>
</body>
</html>
```

For this simple example, we placed the CSS code inside the `style` tag on the same HTML file; don't do that in production.

How to do it...

1. Now we can create our modal directive with the following code:

   ```
   // Creating a simple Modal Directive
   app = angular.module('SimpleModal', []);

   app.directive('modalWindow', function() {
     return {
   ```

```
      restrict: 'E',
      scope: {
        show: '='
      },
      replace: true, // Replace with template
      transclude: true, // To use custom content
      link: function(scope, element, attrs) {

        scope.windowStyle = {};

        if (attrs.width) {
          scope.windowStyle.width = attrs.width;
        }
        if (attrs.height) {
          scope.windowStyle.height = attrs.height;
        }

        scope.hideModal = function() {
          scope.show = false;
        };
      },
      template: "<div ng-show='show'><div class='modal-
        overlay' ng-click='hideModal()'></div><div
        class='modal-background' ng-style='windowStyle'><div
        class='modal-close' ng-click='hideModal()'>X</div><div
        class='modal-content' ng-transclude></div></div></div>"
    };
  });
```

2. Add the controller's code:

```
app.controller('ModalCtrl', ['$scope',
  function($scope) {
    $scope.modalShown = false;
    $scope.toggleModal = function() {
      $scope.modalShown = !$scope.modalShown;
    };
  }
]);
```

3. Finally, include the directives tags into the body tag of our HTML file:

```
<div ng-controller='ModalCtrl'>
  <button ng-click='toggleModal()'>Open Modal</button>
  <modal-window show='modalShown' width='400px'
  height='60%'>
  <p>Hello Simple Modal Window<p>
  </modal-window>
</div>
```

How it works...

The work here is very simple; we just placed an HTML template using the inline template, as we did in the previous example:

```
template: "<div ng-show='show'><div class='modal-overlay' ng-click='hideModal()'></div><div class='modal-background' ng-style='windowStyle'><div class='modal-close' ng-click='hideModal()'>X</div><div class='modal-content' ng-transclude></div></div></div>"
```

As we build everything from scratch, we need to style the HTML tags with CSS classes for a better look using the `style` tag inside the `head` element. In production applications, you must have a separated file for CSS styles.

The inline template contains the built-in directives `ng-show()` and `ng-style()`, along with a `ng-click()` function to hide the modal.

The `ng-style()` directive is not used often, but we include it in this example just to illustrate how we can place inline styles inside a directive.

Inline templates are very useful, but not too flexible. On large application managers, different inline templates can be very painful to use and take a lot of time. Use them with small templates. In the next recipe, we will see how to use external templates on custom directives.

There's more...

We can also use the `ng-transclude` in-built directive to remove any content from the DOM before the modal content inserted.

See also

> - You can read more about the use of `ng-transclude` from the AngularJS official documentation at https://docs.angularjs.org/api/ng/directive/ngTransclude

Loading external templates for best practices

Thinking in terms of best practices, let's see how to use the same modal directive with an external template, using the `templateUrl` property instead of the `template` property. Before we go further, let's explore the two ways to use templates.

Dealing with Modal and Tabs Directives

Use the `script` tag of `ng-template`, as shown in the following example:

```html
<body ng-app='SimpleModal'>
  <script type="text/ng-template" id="modal.html">
  <div ng-show='show'>
    <div class='modal-overlay' ng-click='hideModal()'></div>
    <div class='modal-background' ng-style='windowStyle'>
      <div class='modal-close' ng-click='hideModal()'>X</div>
      <div class='modal-content' ng-transclude></div>
    </div>
  </div>
  </script>
</body>
```

Alternatively, place the HTML content in a separate file; in this case, the template will be an external file, not just external from the directive code. The code is as follows:

```html
<body ng-app='SimpleModal'>
  <div ng-controller='ModalCtrl'>
    <button ng-click='toggleModal()'>Open Modal</button>
    <modal-window show='modalShown' width='400px' height='60%'>
      <p>Hello Simple Modal Window with External Template<p>
    </modal-window>
  </div>
</body>
```

Both ways have the same result, and we will see the difference later. For now, let's focus on the HTML template.

Getting ready

For this recipe, we will be using the same code base as the previous recipe.

How to do it...

1. Let's replace the entire template string with the following code:

   ```js
   // loading external templates
   app = angular.module('SimpleModal', []);

   app.directive('modalWindow', function() {
     return {
       restrict: 'E',
       scope: {
         show: '='
       },
   ```

Chapter 1

```
      replace: true, // Replace with template
      transclude: true, // To use custom content
      link: function(scope, element, attrs) {

        scope.windowStyle = {};

        if (attrs.width) {
          scope.windowStyle.width = attrs.width;
        }
        if (attrs.height) {
          scope.windowStyle.height = attrs.height;
        }

        scope.hideModal = function() {
          scope.show = false;
        };
      },
      templateUrl: "modal.html"
    };
  });
```

2. Remember that we keep the same controller code as the previous example. The `templateUrl` property points to an external file, so place the following code in a blank HTML file and save it as `modal.html`:

```
<body ng-app='SimpleModal'>
  <div ng-controller='ModalCtrl'>
    <button ng-click='toggleModal()'>Open Modal</button>
    <modal-window show='modalShown' width='400px'
    height='60%'>
      <p>Hello Simple Modal Window with External
      Template<p>
    </modal-window>
  </div>
</body>
```

How it works...

With the `templateUrl` property, we can load an external HTML template inside our current HTML file. It is very useful to use this practice because we can reuse the same template in different places in the application. We will cover this topic later on in this book.

 To load external templates inside your files, you must have a HTTP server.

Dealing with Modal and Tabs Directives

There's more...

When we use `type=text/ng-template` with the `script` tag, we need to place the modal content inside our page, and the content will be hidden by the browser. The `script` tag is used to tell the browser that there is a code snippet, usually in JavaScript. In this way, the content of the tag is interpreted differently by the browser. In our case, the `type` attribute indicates that we have a template, as we can see in the previous example.

We can use the same example, as shown in the following code:

```html
<!DOCTYPE html>
<html>
<head>
<script src="https://ajax.googleapis.com/ajax/libs/angularjs/1.3.x/angular.js"></script>
<title>Modal Window Directive</title>
<style>
...
</style>
</head>
<body ng-app='SimpleModal'>
  <script type="text/ng-template" id="modal.html">
    <div ng-controller='ModalCtrl'>
      <button ng-click='toggleModal()'>Open Modal</button>
      <modal-window show='modalShown' width='400px' height='60%'>
        <p>Hello Simple Modal Window using ng-template<p>
      </modal-window>
    </div>
  </script>
</body>
</html>
```

See also

- We also recommend reading the `ng-include` documentation. As we are talking about HTML templates, you can find more information at `https://docs.angularjs.org/api/ng/directive/ngInclude`.

Chapter 1

Using the link function

Now let's take a look at the `link` function property inside the directive. The template generated by a directive is meaningless unless it is compiled with the appropriate scope. Thus, by default, a directive does not get a new child scope. Instead, it is related to the parent scope. This means that if the directive is present within a controller, then it will use this controller scope instead of creating a new one.

To use this scope, we need to use the `link` function. We achieve this by using the `link` property inside the directive definition. Let's use a basic example to understand this.

Getting ready

Let's place the following code inside a new blank HTML file:

```
<!DOCTYPE html>
<html ng-app="linkdirectives">

  <head>
  <script src="https://ajax.googleapis.com/ajax/libs/angularjs/1.2.4/
angular.js"></script>
  <title>Link Function Directive</title>
  </head>

  <body ng-controller="LinkCtrl">
    <input type="text" ng-model="colorName" placeholder="Insert a
color name"/>
    <link-function></link-function>
  </body>

</html>
```

Now let's add the directive code.

How to do it...

Here's the directive code, using simple CSS manipulation:

```
app.directive('linkFunction',function(){
  return{
    restrict: 'AE',
    replace: true,
    template: '<p style="background-color:{{colorName}}">Link
    Function Directive</p>',
```

11

Dealing with Modal and Tabs Directives

```
      link: function(scope,element,attribute){
        element.bind('click',function(){
          element.css('background-color','white');
          scope.$apply(function(){
            scope.color="white";
          });
        });
        element.bind('mouseover',function(){
          element.css('cursor','pointer');
        });
      }
    }
  });
```

How it works...

The `link` function takes three arguments: `scope`, `element`, and `attribute`. For a better understanding, we use the entire name for the arguments, without any abbreviation. It is also very common to see `elem` for `element` and `attrs` for `attribute`.

The `element` argument is a short version from jQuery Lite that is already included in AngularJS to manipulate the DOM without the need to use the famous `$()` from jQuery.

 AngularJS has a lightweight version of jQuery, called **jQuery Lite**.

The `scope` element is the same from the parent controller, and the `link` function is used for attaching event listeners to DOM elements. Always watch the model properties for changes, and update the DOM with the new information. In this case, we used the `$apply()` function to update the binding.

There's more...

The `link` function contains code used after the compilation process, such as some DOM manipulation or jQuery use. Also, the controller `$scope` and `scope` of the `link` function are almost the same thing.

When you use the `scope` element as the first parameter of the `link` function inside a directive, it has the same behavior of the `$scope` element from a controller. However, when you declare the `scope: {}` property with an empty object inside the directive, you create an isolate scope and both are different. We will see more about isolate scopes in the next chapter.

The controller $scope are parameters that are sent to the controller and they get there through **Dependency Injection** (**DI**). The scope of the link function are parameters sent to link and are standard order-based functions.

See also

- You can read more about the Directive Definition Object, Compile, and Link function on the official AngularJS API at https://docs.angularjs.org/api/ng/service/$compile#directive-definition-object

Dealing with tabs without Bootstrap UI directives

Bootstrap user interface is very popular and is used by many web developers. The AngularJS community has their own in-built version on top of the Bootstrap JavaScript library, the AngularJS UI directives. However, using it is not always our first option; often, we need a simple solution.

In this recipe, we will see how to build component tabs without Angular UI.

Later in the book, we will see in depth how to use and customize Bootstrap UI directives. Now, we will focus on a simple directive tabs.

In a very basic way, we don't need to use a custom directive to build the tabs. So, let's see two ways to build a simple tab.

Getting ready

For the first example, we need the following code:

```html
<!DOCTYPE html>
<html ng-app="simpleTab">
<head>
  <script
  src="https://ajax.googleapis.com/ajax/libs/angularjs/1.2.4/
  angular.js"></script>
  <title>Simple tab</title>
  <style>
    .tabs-nav {
      padding: 20px 0 0;
      list-style: none;
    }
    .tabs-nav li {
      display: inline;
```

```
      margin-right: 20px;
    }
    .tabs-nav a {
      display:inline-block;
      cursor: pointer;
    }
    .tabs-nav .active {
      color: red;
    }
    .tab-content {
      border: 1px solid #ddd;
      padding: 20px;
    }
  </style>
</head>

<div class="tabs-holder" ng-app="simpleTab" ng-init="tab=1">
  <ul class="tabs-nav">
    <li><a ng-click="tab=1" ng-class="{'active' : tab==1}">First
    tab</a></li>
    <li><a ng-click="tab=2" ng-class="{'active' : tab==2}">Second
    tab</a></li>
    <li><a ng-click="tab=3" ng-class="{'active' : tab==3}">Third
    tab</a></li>
  </ul>

  <div class="tabs-container">
    <div class="tab-content" ng-show="tab == 1">
      <h1>First Tab</h1>
      <p>Simple tab 1</p>
    </div>
    <div class="tab-content" ng-show="tab == 2">
      <h1>Second tab</h1>
      <p>Simple tab 2</p>
    </div>

    <div class="tab-content" ng-show="tab == 3">
      <h1>Third Tab</h1>
      <p>Simple tab 3</p>
    </div>
  </div>
</div>
</body>
</html>
```

Chapter 1

For the second example, we need the following code. This time, we're using a controller and an external template. Place the following HTML code in a blank HTML file:

```html
<!DOCTYPE html>
<html ng-app="simpleTabController">
<head>
  <script
  src="https://ajax.googleapis.com/ajax/libs/angularjs/1.2.4/
  angular.js"></script>
  <title>Simple tab with Controller</title>
  <style>
    .tabs-nav {
      padding: 20px 0 0;
      list-style: none;
    }
    .tabs-nav li {
      display: inline;
      margin-right: 20px;
    }
    .tabs-nav a {
      display:inline-block;
      cursor: pointer;
    }
    .tabs-nav .active {
      color: red;
    }
    .tab-content {
      border: 1px solid #ddd;
      padding: 20px;
    }
  </style>
</head>
<body>
<div class="tabs-holder" ng-app="simpleTabController">
<div id="tabs" ng-controller="TabsCtrl">
  <ul class="tabs-nav">
    <li ng-repeat="tab in tabs"
    ng-class="{active:isActiveTab(tab.url)}"
    ng-click="onClickTab(tab)">{{tab.title}}</li>
  </ul>
  <div id="tab-content">
    <div ng-include="currentTab"></div>
  </div>
  <!--Script templates-->
```

[15]

Dealing with Modal and Tabs Directives

```html
<script type="text/ng-template" id="first.html">
  <div class="tab-content" id="1">
    <h1>First Tab</h1>
    <p>Simple tab 1</p>
  </div>
</script>

<script type="text/ng-template" id="second.html">
  <div class="tab-content" id="2">
    <h1>Second Tab</h1>
    <p>Simple tab 2</p>
  </div>
</script>

<script type="text/ng-template" id="third.html">
  <div class="tab-content" id="3">
    <h1>Third Tab</h1>
    <p>Simple tab 3</p>
  </div>
</script>
    </div>
  </div>
</body>
</html>
```

How to do it...

With the HTML already set up for both examples, let's dive into the controller's code for the second one. Add the following code to a separate file:

```js
angular.module('simpleTabController', [])

.controller('TabsCtrl', ['$scope', function ($scope) {
  $scope.tabs = [{
    title: 'First tab',
    url: 'first.html'
  }, {
    title: 'Second tab',
    url: 'second.html'
  }, {
    title: 'Third tab',
    url: 'third.html'
  }];
```

```
    $scope.currentTab = 'first.html';

    $scope.onClickTab = function (tab) {
      $scope.currentTab = tab.url;
    }

    $scope.isActiveTab = function(tabUrl) {
      return tabUrl == $scope.currentTab;
    }
}]);
```

The result of the tabs example is very similar to the following screenshot:

Simple tab layout example

Note that we keep the layout as simple as possible just for the example code.

For the second example, we keep the same stylesheet and layout. In both the examples, we include the CSS inside the `head` element on the HTML page; you must avoid this on production applications.

Dealing with Modal and Tabs Directives

How it works...

The first example is pretty intuitive, and we only use the AngularJS built-in directives, such as `ng-class` and `ng-show`, to simulate the tab functionality.

```
<ul class="tabs-nav">
  <li><a ng-click="tab=1" ng-class="{'active' : tab==1}">First
  tab</a></li>
  <li><a ng-click="tab=2" ng-class="{'active' : tab==2}">Second
  tab</a></li>
  <li><a ng-click="tab=3" ng-class="{'active' : tab==3}">Third
  tab</a></li>
</ul>
```

Internally, the framework recognizes the reverse state of `ng-show` and hides all the content of tabs 1 and 2. When we click on one of the other tabs, the state changes to show what has been clicked on and hides the others.

This is a simple example, but it is not very flexible.

In the second example, we added a controller to deal with the tabs logic, creating a `$scope` to hold the tab title and their respective template:

```
$scope.tabs = [{
  title: 'First tab',
  url: 'first.html'
}, {
  title: 'Second tab',
  url: 'second.html'
}, {
  title: 'Third tab',
  url: 'third.html'
}];
```

We could easily introduce other elements in this array, such as description, date, and other elements, since we have loaded them from the controller. Although, it is possible to load the tabs content dynamically within this own array. We can also load the templates in external files, as we saw in the beginning of this chapter.

For this, transfer the contents of the `script` tags (highlighted here) to external files, keeping the names as `first.html`, `second.html`, and `third.html`:

```
<script type="text/ng-template" id="first.html">
  <div class="tab-content" id="1">
    <h1>First Tab</h1>
    <p>Simple tab 1</p>
  </div>
</script>
```

Now just remove the `script` tags from the original HTML file:

```html
<script type="text/ng-template" id="second.html">
  <div class="tab-content" id="2">
    <h1>Second Tab</h1>
    <p>Simple tab 2</p>
  </div>
</script>

<script type="text/ng-template" id="third.html">
  <div class="tab-content" id="3">
    <h1>Third Tab</h1>
    <p>Simple tab 3</p>
  </div>
</script>
```

Now we can have tabs with external templates.

These were simple examples for creation of tabs without using custom directives, and instead using built-in AngularJS directives. We highlighted the DOM manipulation's simplicity by using controllers rather than customized directives.

There's more...

In addition to the previous examples, we can easily create a directive to use tabs. So, we address all the possibilities in the creation of this interactive component.

Let's see a directive example:

```html
<!DOCTYPE html>
<html >
<head>
  <script src="https://ajax.googleapis.com/ajax/libs/angularjs/1.2.4/angular.js"></script>
  <title>Simple tab with Directive</title>
  <style>
    .tabs-nav {
      padding: 20px 0 0;
      list-style: none;
    }
    .tabs-nav li {
      display: inline;
      margin-right: 20px;
    }
```

```
      .tabs-nav a {
        display:inline-block;
        cursor: pointer;
      }
      .tabs-nav .active {
        color: red;
      }
      .tab-content {
        border: 1px solid #ddd;
        padding: 20px;
      }
    </style>
  </head>
  <body>
    <div ng-app='simpleTabDirective'>
      <ng-tabs>
        <content-tab dat-heading='First tab' dat-tab-active>
          <h1>First Tab</h1>
          <p>Simple tab 1</p>
        </content-tab>
        <content-tab dat-heading='Second tab'>
          <h1>Second Tab</h1>
          <p>Simple tab 2</p>
        </content-tab>
        <content-tab dat-heading='Third tab'>
          <h1>Third Tab</h1>
          <p>Simple tab 3</p>
        </content-tab>
      </ng-tabs>
    </div>
  </body>
</html>
```

Now, the controller turns into a directive:

```
var app = angular.module("simpleTabDirective", [])

app.directive('ngTabs', function() {
  return {
    scope: true,
    replace: true,
    restrict: 'E',
    transclude: true,
    template: ' \
```

```
<div class="tab-content"> \
  <ul class="tabs-nav"> \
    <li ng-repeat="tab in tabs" \
        ng-class="{ active: currentTab == $index }"> \
      <a ng-click="selectTab($index)"> \
        {{tab}} \
      </a> \
    </li> \
  </ul> \
  <div ng-transclude></div> \
</div>',
    controller: function($scope) {
      $scope.currentTab = 0;

      $scope.tabs = [];

      $scope.selectTab = function(index) {
        $scope.currentTab = index;
      };

      return $scope;
    }
  }
})

app.directive('contentTab', function() {
  return {
    require: '^ngTabs',
    restrict: 'E',
    transclude: true,
    replace: true,
    scope: true,
    template: '<div class="tab-content" ng-show="showTab()" ng-transclude></div>',
    link: function(scope, element, attrs, ngTabs) {
      var tabId = ngTabs.tabs.length;

      scope.showTab = function() {
        return tabId == ngTabs.currentTab;
      };

      ngTabs.tabs.push(attrs.datHeading);
    }
  }
});
```

Dealing with Modal and Tabs Directives

Note that we use the property `require` to set the dependence of `ngTabs`. In this way, our tab consists of two directives, one to create the list where we will have the title of the tabs and the second to create the contents of each tab itself. The code is as follows:

```
<ng-tabs>
  <content-tab dat-heading='First tab'>
  </content-tab>
</ng-tabs>
```

We can also observe that we have used all the features seen earlier in this chapter, such as `ng-click`, `ng-repeat`, and `ng-transclude`, among others.

See also

- A great resource that helps us in search of directives, and other related stuff, for the development of applications with AngularJS is the website Angular Modules (http://ngmodules.org/tags/directive)

2
Building a Navbar Custom Directive

In this chapter, we will cover:

- Building a navbar directive
- Directory structure for common components
- Directive's controller function
- Using the data attribute to HTML5 compile

Introduction

In this chapter, we will see how to build a `navbar` directive and adapt it to an AngularJS application. We will also explore some basic functionalities of AngularJS directives. We will use a Yeoman generator to facilitate our work and illustrate how to organize your directory structure following the AngularJS best practices from the community.

It is assumed that you have an intermediate knowledge of developing applications using AngularJS and modern tools such as Yeoman, Bower, and Grunt. However, the following examples are exemplified didactically.

> You can find more information about Yeoman at `http://yeoman.io/`.

Building a Navbar Custom Directive

Building a navbar directive

One of the interface components most commonly used on websites and web applications are navigation menus. Although they are very simple, they are also very useful in any type of application.

Getting ready

Let's build the basis for an AngularJS application. As we mentioned before, we use the Yeoman generator: `generator-angm`.

> You must have Node.js, Yeoman, Bower, and Grunt already installed on your machine.

Open your Terminal window and type the following commands in the order they appear:

1. To install the generator, use the following command:

   `npm install generator-angm -g`

2. To create the application, use the following command:

   `yo angm`

3. To create the modules, use the following command:

   `yo angm:angm-module`

4. Use the name `about` for the module name.

   Repeat the last step to create the following modules: `news`, `company`, and `navbar`. We will discuss this in detail later.

5. Now, test the boilerplate code. On your Terminal, type the following command:

   `grunt dev`

All the code will be compiled and your default browser will start with the welcome screen.

> Remember, you must have administrator privileges to install the generator globally on your machine.

After all these commands have been executed, we'll have created all the necessary directory structures for the directive example. At this point, you should have a directory structure similar to the following screenshot:

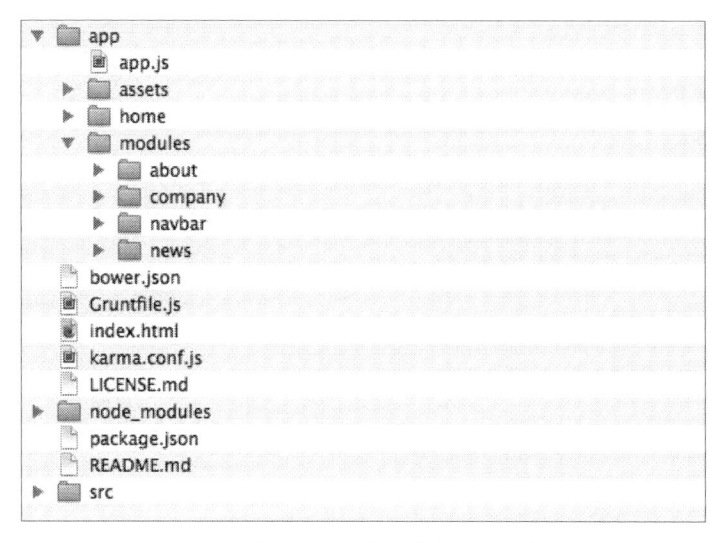

```
▼ 📁 app
    📄 app.js
  ▶ 📁 assets
  ▶ 📁 home
  ▼ 📁 modules
    ▶ 📁 about
    ▶ 📁 company
    ▶ 📁 navbar
    ▶ 📁 news
  📄 bower.json
  📄 Gruntfile.js
  📄 index.html
  📄 karma.conf.js
  📄 LICENSE.md
▶ 📁 node_modules
  📄 package.json
  📄 README.md
▶ 📁 src
```

Generator-angm with modules created

The generator has created all the necessary code of an AngularJS application, following the best development practices. However, we will not go into detail about all these files, as it is beyond the scope of this book.

Let's focus on the `navbar` folder and start building our `navbar` directive. The `navbar` folder has the following files:

Filename	Description
`navabar-test.js`	Unity tests related to the navbar module controller
`navbar.html`	Navbar view for the navbar module
`navbarCtrl.js`	Navbar controller
`navbarRoute.js`	AngularJS Route to Navbar view

Aside from the unit test file and the route file, the additional files are blank and just have the function declarations.

Building a Navbar Custom Directive

How to do it...

1. We will replace the file `navbarRoute.js` with `navbarDirective.js`. For a better understanding, we will follow these steps. Place the following code inside the `navbarDirective.js` file:

   ```
   'use strict';

   /**
    * @ngdoc function
    * @name app.directive:navbarDirective
    * @description
    * # navbarDirective
    * Directive of the app
    */

   angular.module('navbar')
     .directive('simpleNavbar', function () {
       return {
         restrict: 'E',
         templateUrl: 'app/modules/navbar/navbar.html',
         controller: function($scope, $location) {
           $scope.isActive = function(path){
             var currentPath = $location.path().split('/')[1];
             if (currentPath.indexOf('?') !== -1) {
               currentPath = currentPath.split('?')[0];
             }
             return currentPath === path.split('/')[1];
           };
         },
       };
     });
   ```

2. Place the following HTML code inside the `navbar.html` file:

   ```
   <div class="navbar navbar-default">
     <div class="container">
       <ul class="nav navbar-nav">
         <li ng-class="{active:isActive('/')}"><a
         href="#!/">Home</a></li>
         <li ng-class="{active:isActive('#/about')}"><a
         href="#!/about">About</a></li>
         <li ng-class="{active:isActive('#/news')}"><a
         href="#!/news">News</a></li>
   ```

```
      <li ng-class="{active:isActive('#/company')}"><a
      href="#!/company">Company</a></li>
    </ul>
  </div>
</div>
```

3. At this stage, we have almost everything we need to build the directive. The final step is to add the `navbar` directive inside the HTML file. Open the `index.html` file inside the project root folder and add the following highlighted code to the markup:

```
<!--Beginning-->
<!-- Insert the Navbar -->
<simple-navbar></simple-navbar>
<section id="wrapper" class="container" scroll-to>
  <div class="view-slide-in" ng-view="main-app"></div>
</section>
<!--End-->
```

4. Now, open your Terminal window and type the following command:

   grunt dev

At this point, the code has been compiled and your default browser will have opened on the welcome screen with the `navbar` directive on the top of the page, as shown in the following screenshot:

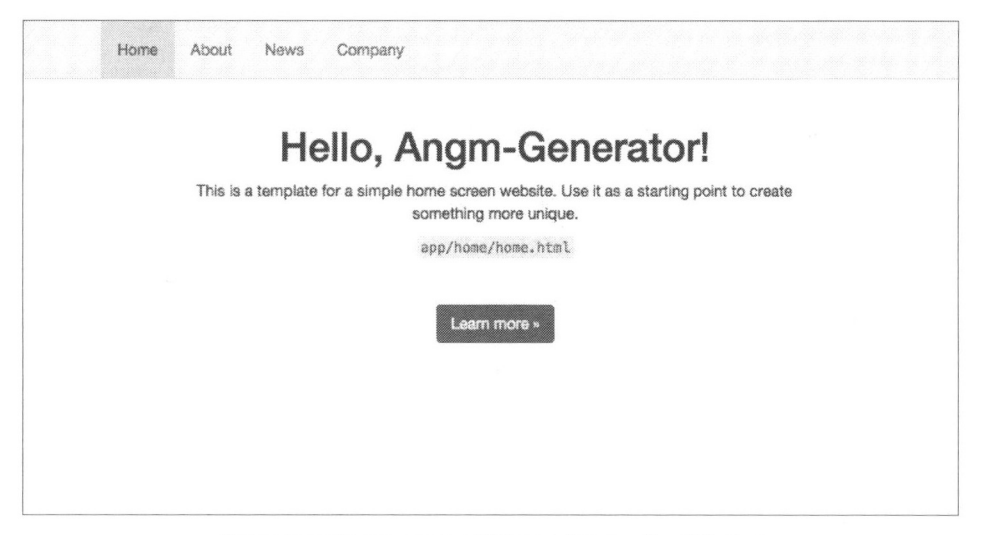

Generator welcome screen with the navbar directive at the top

Building a Navbar Custom Directive

How it works...

As you've probably noticed, there are several ways to create custom directives with AngularJS. The key point here is to understand all the basic concepts behind directives creation.

The controller only checks the link state and returns a state if it is active with a route using the `$location.path()` function. The code is as follows:

```
$scope.isActive = function(path){
  var currentPath = $location.path().split('/')[1];
  if (currentPath.indexOf('?') !== -1) {
    currentPath = currentPath.split('?')[0];
  }
  return currentPath === path.split('/')[1];
};
```

The template gets the state from the controller and applies the selected CSS class to the link using the `ng-class` built-in directive. The code is as follows:

```
<li ng-class="{active:isActive('/')}"><a href="#!/">Home</a></li>
<li ng-class="{active:isActive('#/about')}"><a href="#!/about">About</a></li>
li ng-class="{active:isActive('#/news')}"><a href="#!/news">News</a></li>
<li ng-class="{active:isActive('#/company')}"><a href="#!/company">Company</a></li>
```

All this happens inside the directive markup:

```
<simple-navbar></simple-navbar>
```

There's more...

An important point to note is that the generator compiles and injects all the code of `controllers`, `routes`, and `directives` in the `index.html` file, as we can see in the following code:

```
<script src="/app/app.js"></script>
<script src="/app/home/homeRoute.js"></script>
<script src="/app/modules/about/aboutRoute.js"></script>
<script src="/app/modules/company/companyRoute.js"></script>
<script src="/app/modules/news/newsRoute.js"></script>
<script src="/app/home/homeCtrl.js"></script>
<script src="/app/modules/about/aboutCtrl.js"></script>
<script src="/app/modules/company/companyCtrl.js"></script>
```

Building a Navbar Custom Directive

We will use the same code base for the previous recipe to explain the benefits of this kind of organization. The following screenshot shows a directory structure grouped by features:

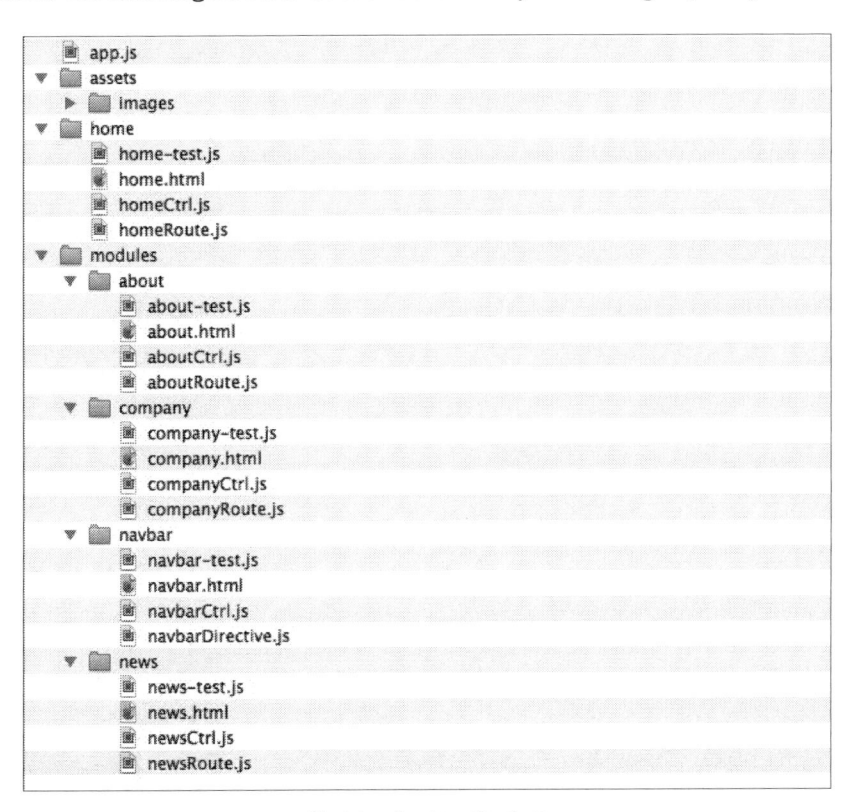

```
app.js
assets
    images
home
    home-test.js
    home.html
    homeCtrl.js
    homeRoute.js
modules
    about
        about-test.js
        about.html
        aboutCtrl.js
        aboutRoute.js
    company
        company-test.js
        company.html
        companyCtrl.js
        companyRoute.js
    navbar
        navbar-test.js
        navbar.html
        navbarCtrl.js
        navbarDirective.js
    news
        news-test.js
        news.html
        newsCtrl.js
        newsRoute.js
```

Modular directory structure

How to do it...

You should group your modules into folders and put all content on that functionality within these folders.

For example, in the previous screenshot, we have a folder called `modules` and each feature has its own folder, such as `news`, `navbar`, `company`, and so on.

Controllers, Routes, Directives, Services, stylesheets, and everything that is related to the contents of the folder and functionality, should have individual folders.

When we use some kind of generator or boilerplate, we can easily opt for one that lets the best structured code. In many cases, this becomes unfeasible, for example, in the case of applications in progress where the code was not properly structured.

```
<script src="/app/modules/navbar/navbarCtrl.js"></script>
<script src="/app/modules/news/newsCtrl.js"></script>
<script src="/app/modules/navbar/navbarDirective.js"></script>
```

If you are creating this directive without using a generator, you need to be aware of this step. Otherwise, your code may return an injection of dependencies error.

You must have also noticed that we do not use any CSS to style our `navbar`. This is because the generator includes a copy of the Twitter bootstrap framework and we only use the already available classes from the framework.

```
<div class="navbar navbar-default">
  <div class="container">
    ...
  </div>
</div>
```

See also

You can use any user interface framework with AngularJS. However, you must create its own directives to use JavaScript behavior and DOM manipulation in AngularJS applications. Some user interface frameworks, such as Foundation and Bootstrap, have specific directives to AngularJS.

We will see more on this subject later in this book.

Directory structure for common components

A very useful way to develop applications with AngularJS is to use a code generator, use a simple Boilerplate, or to create your own generator or guidelines to follow. We have a lot of good practices spreading on the Internet. However, you should find your own way too.

We often need to write enough code to have a fast start, and putting a simple application in production requires many lines of code, so using tools like generators can be very productive. However, let's see some tips on how to organize our code in order to have a highly scalable application.

Getting ready

Regardless of a code generator or boilerplate, you should choose to organize your content in a modular way by grouping by features. Grouping files by features facilitates maintenance and allows you to scale the application more easily.

Unfortunately, at the beginning of development with AngularJS, it was very common to use the directories structure grouped by function, that is, all controllers, services, routes and directives of the application were grouped into folders, each folder for a feature. For example, a controller's folder would be grouped with all application controllers.

Over time, this has become a problem, especially in teams where all developers need to maintain the code. The tree files always tend to grow, and the organization by functionality is much better than by function.

How it works...

As a simple way to structure an application, you can make an analogy with building blocks.

All applications with AngularJS have files and features in common. Some behaviors and components also tend to be very similar to many types of web applications with login screens, registration, forms, and much more.

A simple way to solve this is to use the following figure as a guide for implementing a well-organized structure that is easy to scale:

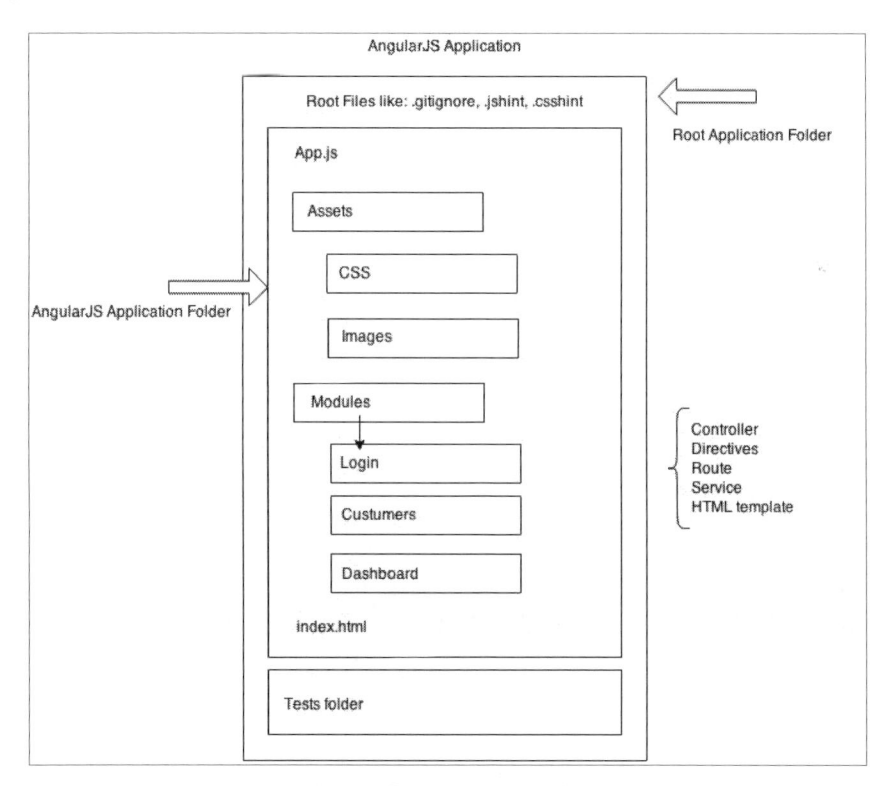

AngularJS application blueprint

Building a Navbar Custom Directive

Also, some IDE tools are very helpful when we need to perform massive code refactoring. For the directives, it's always a good practice to have an extra folder inside the module folder to hold all the directives assets and templates. This is shown in the following figure:

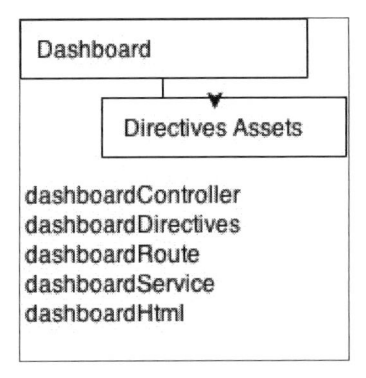

```
Dashboard
    |
    v
    Directives Assets

dashboardController
dashboardDirectives
dashboardRoute
dashboardService
dashboardHtml
```

Dashboard module detail

In this way, it is very easy to delete and add new modules, using only a single directory from the entire application and using a `config` file to add the modules' dependencies. In this case, we just need to delete the folder's name and remove the module injection on the `config` file. Also, we can delete all the references to the module on the application.

There's more...

Avoid using prefixes already used by other AngularJS directives, for example, `ng-` or `ui-`. The first one is dedicated to all the Angular built-in directives and the second one is for Angular UI Bootstrap directives.

Name your directives in the most intuitive way possible and follow the camelCase naming convention; keeping short names is better.

See also

- In *Chapter 3, Customizing and Using Bootstrap UI Directives*, we will discuss more on directives naming conventions.

Directive's controller function

In this chapter, we have seen a different way to declare a directive to manipulate the DOM. In the previous chapter, we explored different ways of working with the directive's properties. In this example, we will declare an external controller to the directive without writing any code within the directive.

― Chapter 2

Getting ready

Using external controllers is very common in applications that have many customized directives. They help us separate the content in a more practical way, in the same behavior of the directives template. With separated controllers, we can use many AngularJS resources, such as services and other features.

This example serves to illustrate the flexibility that directives have.

We will use the same code as the previous example, but this time, we will place the controller's code in a separate file.

How to do it...

1. Replace the controller's code with the following highlighted code:

   ```
   'use strict';

   /**
    * @ngdoc function
    * @name app.directive:navbarDirective
    * @description
    * # navbarDirective
    * Directive of the app
    */

   angular.module('navbar')
     .directive('simpleNavbar', function () {
       return {
         restrict: 'E',
         templateUrl: 'app/modules/navbar/navbar.html',
         controller: 'NavbarCtrl',
       };
   });
   ```

2. Create a navbarCtrl.js file and place the following code in it:

   ```
   'use strict';

   /**
    * @ngdoc function
    * @name app.controller:navbarCtrl
    * @description
    * # navbarCtrl
    * Controller of the app
   ```

Building a Navbar Custom Directive

```
     */
    angular.module('navbar')
    .controller('NavbarCtrl', ['$scope', '$location', function
    ($scope, $location) {
      $scope.isActive = function(path){
        var currentPath = $location.path().split('/')[1];
        if (currentPath.indexOf('?') !== -1) {
          currentPath = currentPath.split('?')[0];
        }
        return currentPath === path.split('/')[1];
      };
    }]);
```

How it works...

We used a different approach on this directive. Note that we declared our controller in a separate file, called `navbarCtrl.js`, unlike what we did in the previous example.

> Note that some linter tools ask you to name your controller without the abbreviation `Ctrl` at the end of the controller's name, so consider using `navbarController.js` on production applications.

The operation is very simple: just declare the controller name that will be used. It should be in the same directory of the directive code.

In our previous example, we can see that the directives should have their own directory in large AngularJS applications, and that all relevant files for the directive are stored in this directory.

In our case, the controller has the same name as the directive. It is stored on the same `navbar` folder, `NavbarDirective.js`.

There's more...

An important note is the method used to declare the contents of the controller and directives. Let's see some key points:

```
'use strict';

/**
 * @ngdoc function
 * @name app.controller:navbarCtrl
 * @description
```

```
 * # navbarCtrl
 * Controller of the app
 */
angular.module('navbar')
.controller('NavbarCtrl', ['$scope', '$location', function
($scope, $location) {
  ...


}]);
```

We are using an `array []` notation to declare the dependencies. Using only functions can lead to some issues when we try to minify and obfuscate the file. One of the common ways to see this is like the following example:

```
function navBarCtrl ($scope, $location) {
...
...
}
```

This code easily loses its parameters, `$scope` and `$location`, when minified because they are turned into `(a,b)` by some minify tools.

See also

> A very good resource to know more about controllers in AngularJS applications is the official documentation at `https://docs.angularjs.org/guide/controller`

Using the data attribute to HTML5 compile

The `data` attribute is an important and powerful feature of HTML5. It helps us to have more control over the HTML of our application, and this is not different on AngularJS applications.

Imagine that you are working on an AngularJS application and need to validate your HTML with a validating tool. Many companies require that you ensure your HTML code is valid, by quality questions or web standards, and others simply use it as a selling point for future customers.

If you try to validate an AngularJS application, it will have some or many errors related to the `ng-` tags. To avoid this, we must use the following solution.

Building a Navbar Custom Directive

Getting ready

Let's use the same `navbar` HTML code from the previous example to show the use of the `data` attribute.

How to do it...

1. Just apply the `data-` attribute before all the `ng-` tags:

   ```
   <div class="navbar navbar-default">
     <div class="container">
       <ul class="nav navbar-nav">
         <li data-ng-class="{active:isActive('/')}"><a
         href="#!/">Home</a></li>
         <li data-ng-class="{active:isActive('#/about')}"><a
         href="#!/about">About</a></li>
         <li data-ng-class="{active:isActive('#/news')}"><a
         href="#!/news">News</a></li>
         <li data-ng-class="{active:isActive('#/company')}"><a
         href="#!/company">Company</a></li>
       </ul>
     </div>
   </div>
   ```

2. Apply the `data-` attribute to the directives name:

   ```
   <data-simple-navbar></data-simple-navbar>
   ```

How it works...

When the browser's engine parses the HTML code, it'll understand the `data-` tag as the HTML5 attribute and the validator's engine will pass easily.

There's more...

Almost all updated browsers parsing the `data-` attribute using the `getAttribute` and `setAttribute` methods.

You can easily manipulate the HTML tags with pure JavaScript, as shown in the following example:

```
<div id="band" data-band="Motorhead" data-album="March or
Die"></div>
```

Use the JavaScript in this way:

```
var band = document.getElementById("band");
var bestBand = band.getAttribute("data-band");
var bestAlbum = band.getAttribute("data-album");
console.log('The best band and album is', bestBand + bestAlbum);
```

See also

- You can find more information about data attributes on HTML5 applications at http://www.w3.org/html/wg/drafts/html/master/dom.html#custom-data-attribute

3
Customizing and Using Bootstrap UI Directives

In this chapter, we will cover the following recipes:

- Dealing with modal directives
- Creating tab directives
- The isolate $scope
- Building the accordion tab directives
- Loading dynamic content

Introduction

User interface is the most common part of any web application or even a simple website. Among the most known and used UI frameworks is the Twitter Bootstrap framework. In addition, the AngularJS ecosystem has its own version of Bootstrap, as the website says.

> Statement from the UI-Bootstrap website: Bootstrap components written in pure AngularJS by the AngularUI Team.

Pure AngularJS means custom directives simulate the JavaScript behavior from the original Bootstrap framework. The AngularJS team translated all the Bootstrap components into AngularJS directives and the only dependency is the CSS file, without jQuery.

In this chapter, we will go deeper inside the AngularJS UI directives.

Customizing and Using Bootstrap UI Directives

Dealing with modal directives

As we have already noted in the previous chapters, modal components are extremely common in web applications or even on small websites.

In the upcoming sections, we will show a simple modal solution loading content from a simple controller using the Bootstrap UI, and also an alternative way to extend it using a custom external template demonstrating the flexibility of custom directives with the Bootstrap UI.

Getting ready

As a starting point, we will use the `generator-angm`; the baseline code will be the default home directory.

At this point, we assume that you have the generator installed on your development environment and a project already started.

How to do it...

1. Place the following highlighted code in the `homeCtrl.js` file in the home directory:

```
/**
 * @ngdoc function
 * @name app.controller:HomeCtrl
 * @description
 * # HomeCtrl
 * Controller of the app
 */
angular.module('bootstrap-ui-directives')
// Passing the $modal to controller as dependency
.controller('HomeCtrl', ['$scope', '$modal', function
($scope, $modal) {
  $scope.title = "Hello, Angm-Generator!";

  $scope.open = function () {

    var modalInstance = $modal.open({
      templateUrl: 'myModalContent.html',
      controller: 'ModalCtrl'
    });

  };

}])
```

2. Now, let's add the modal controller. For the example code, we use the same `homeCtrl.js` file to hold all the code examples. However, in production applications, you must, or at least should, have one controller for each goal. Let's go to the second step and add the `ModaCtrl` function:

```
// Passing $modalInstance to controller as dependency
.controller('ModalCtrl', function ($scope, $modalInstance) {

  // Added some content to Modal using $scope
  $scope.content = "ModalCtrl, Yeah!"

  // Add cancel button
  $scope.cancel = function () {
    $modalInstance.dismiss('cancel');
  };
})
```

3. Note that we have appended this controller to the `homectrl.js` file. Now, let's add the modal HTML content to the `home.html` file inside the home directory. Add the following highlighted code:

```
<div ng-controller="HomeCtrl">
  <div class="splash" style="width:600px; margin:0 auto;
  text-align:center">
      <h1>{{ title }}</h1>
      <p>This is a template for a simple home screen
      website. Use it as a starting point to create
      something more unique.</p>
      <code>app/home/home.html</code>
      <hr>
      <p><a ng-click="open()" class="btn btn-primary"
      role="button">Open Modal »</a></p>
  </div>
  <!-- Modal Script -->
  <script type="text/ng-template" id="myModalContent.html">
    <div class="modal-header">
      <button type="button" class="close" data-
      dismiss="modal" aria-hidden="true">&times;</button>
      <h3 class="modal-title">Hello from Modal!</h3>
    </div>
    <div class="modal-body">
      Modal Content from: <b>{{ content }}</b>
    </div>
    <div class="modal-footer">
      <button class="btn btn-danger" ng-
      click="cancel()">Cancel</button>
    </div>
  </script>
</div>
```

4. Note that we have added a custom template to display the modal called `myModalContent.html`. Open your Terminal window inside the application folder and type:

   grunt dev

   The result expected when the modal button is clicked is what we have in the following screenshot:

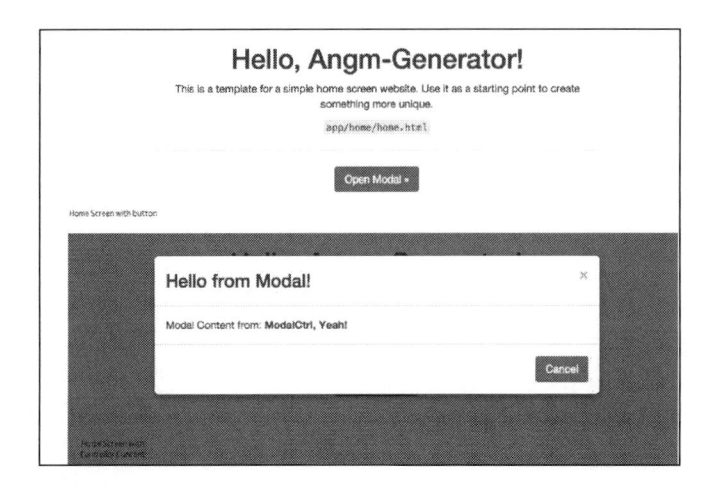

   Home Screen with button

   Modal Screen with Controller Content

5. We can easily extend this functionality by creating a custom directive and an external template, as already mentioned earlier. To do this, perform the following steps and add the following code to your application:

   ```
   .controller('ModalCustomCtrl', function ($scope) {
     // Set show modal to false/ hide from HTML
     $scope.showModal = false;

     // Toggle function to show and hide modal from HTML
     $scope.toggleModal = function(){
       $scope.showModal = !$scope.showModal;
     };
   })
   // Modal Directive
   .directive('modal', function () {
     return {
       // Add a custom template for modal
       templateUrl: 'app/home/modal-tpl.html',
       restrict: 'E',
       transclude: true,
       replace:true,
       scope:true,
   ```

```
      link: function postLink(scope, element, attrs) {
        scope.title = attrs.title;

        scope.$watch(attrs.visible, function(value){
          if(value == true)
            $(element).modal('show');
          else
            $(element).modal('hide');
        });

        $(element).on('shown.bs.modal', function(){
          scope.$apply(function(){
            scope.$parent[attrs.visible] = true;
          });
        });

        $(element).on('hidden.bs.modal', function(){
          scope.$apply(function(){
            scope.$parent[attrs.visible] = false;
          });
        });
      }
    };
  })
```

6. As we are extending a directive, we will use an external template called `modal-tpl.html` to demonstrate the flexibility of this directive. Let's add the following HTML code:

```
<div class="modal fade">
  <div class="modal-dialog">
    <div class="modal-content">
      <div class="modal-header">
        <button type="button" class="close" data-
        dismiss="modal" aria-hidden="true">&times;</button>
        <h4 class="modal-title">{{ title }}</h4>
      </div>
      <div class="modal-body" ng-transclude></div>
      <div class="modal-footer">
        <button class="btn btn-danger" data-
        dismiss="modal">Cancel</button>
      </div>
    </div>
  </div>
</div>
```

Customizing and Using Bootstrap UI Directives

How it works...

It is very simple to use the Angular UI Bootstrap components on Angular applications. Note that the generator we use already has Bootstrap installed and configured, though it is very simple to do this.

> You can find more about the Angular Bootstrap UI on the official website at `http://angular-ui.github.io/bootstrap/`.

In the first example, we pass the `$modal` attribute as a parameter to the `HomeCtrl` function and set up the template and controller to hold the modal content:

```
.controller('HomeCtrl', ['$scope', '$modal', function ($scope, $modal)
{
  $scope.title = "Hello, Angm-Generator!";

  $scope.open = function () {

    var modalInstance = $modal.open({
      templateUrl: 'myModalContent.html',
      controller: 'ModalCtrl'
    });
  };
}])
```

The modal controller uses the `$modalInstance` attribute as a parameter and the `$scope` attribute with modal content.

```
.controller('ModalCtrl', function ($scope, $modalInstance) {

  // Added some content to Modal using $scope
  $scope.content = "ModalCtrl, Yeah!"

  // Add cancel button
  $scope.cancel = function () {
    $modalInstance.dismiss('cancel');
  };
})
```

In this example, we only use the Bootstrap built-in directive to enable a modal component. However, we don't have direct contact with the directive's code.

Chapter 3

In the second example, we extended this control and created our own directive called `modal` using a custom template:

```js
// Modal Directive
.directive('modal', function () {
  return {
    // Add a custom template for modal
    templateUrl: 'app/home/modal-tpl.html',
    restrict: 'E',
    transclude: true,
    replace:true,
    scope:true,
    link: function postLink(scope, element, attrs) {
      scope.title = attrs.title;

      scope.$watch(attrs.visible, function(value){
        if(value == true)
          $(element).modal('show');
        else
          $(element).modal('hide');
      });

      $(element).on('shown.bs.modal', function(){
        scope.$apply(function(){
          scope.$parent[attrs.visible] = true;
        });
      });

      $(element).on('hidden.bs.modal', function(){
        scope.$apply(function(){
          scope.$parent[attrs.visible] = false;
        });
      });
    }
  };
})
```

To use it, we only need to declare it in our markup, within the given controller, as shown in the following example:

```html
<!-- Custom Modal -->
<div ng-controller="ModalCustomCtrl">
  <div style="width:600px; margin:0 auto; text-align:center">
    <button ng-click="toggleModal()" class="btn btn-default">Open
    modal custom Directive</button>
```

Customizing and Using Bootstrap UI Directives

```html
    </div>
    <!-- Modal from Custom Directive-->
    <modal title="Modal Custom Directive" visible="showModal">
      Content Modal from: <b>Custom Directive</b>
    </modal>
</div>
```

With just a few lines of code, we have a very flexible custom modal directive.

There's more...

The `ui-bootstrap-tpls.js` file has all the Bootstrap templates inline on the JavaScript file using the `$templateCache` function:

```
angular.module("template/modal/window.html",
[]).run(["$templateCache", function($templateCache) {
  $templateCache.put("template/modal/window.html", "<div
  tabindex=\"-1\" role=\"dialog\" class=\"modal fade\" ng-
  class=\"{in: animate}\" ng-style=\"{'z-index': 1050 + index*10,
  display: 'block'}\" ng-click=\"close($event)\">\n" + " <div
  class=\"modal-dialog\" ng-class=\"{'modal-sm': size == 'sm',
  'modal-lg': size == 'lg'}\"><div class=\"modal-content\" modal-
  transclude></div></div>\n" + "</div>");
}]);
```

> It is also possible to use dynamic content to fill the modal's body content; we will see an example of this in the next topic.

Creating tab directives

In this recipe, we will see how to use another important interface component, Tabs, using the `$http` function to load some content.

Getting ready

To accomplish this task, we will create a controller and use the `get` method of the `$http` function to retrieve the contents of a JSON file, but first, let's create the JSON content.

We are still using the same code base of the previous example.

How to do it...

1. Create a new JSON file and name it `tab-content.json`, and add the following code:

   ```
   [
       {
           "title": "Dynamic Title 1",
           "content": "Dynamic content 1"
       },
       {
           "title": "Dynamic Title 2",
           "content": "Dynamic content 2"
       }
   ]
   ```

2. A simple array with two properties, save the file in the home directory. Append the following code in the `homeCtrl.js` file right after the modal directive:

   ```
   .controller('BootstrapTabCtrl', function ($scope, $http) {

     // Added some content to Tab / can be from a JSON with
     $http or $resource
     $http.get('app/home/tab-content.json').
     success(function(data) {
       // Get dynamic data from JSON file
       $scope.tabs = data;
     }).
     error(function(status) {
       // if error, show status
       console.log(status);
     });
   })
   ```

3. Now, let's add the HTML code to the `home.html` file, right after the modal code:

   ```
   <!-- Bootstrap Tab -->
   <div style="width:600px; margin:20px auto;">
     <div ng-controller="BootstrapTabCtrl">
       <tabset>
         <tab ng-repeat="tab in tabs" heading="{{tab.title}}"
         active="tab.active" disabled="tab.disabled">
         {{tab.content}}
         </tab>
       </tabset>
     </div>
   </div>
   ```

Customizing and Using Bootstrap UI Directives

4. Following the same format as the previous example, we will now create a custom directive to extend the UI Bootstrap functionality:

```
.directive('customTabs', function() {
  return {
    restrict: 'E',
    transclude: true,
    scope: {},
    controller: [ "$scope", function($scope) {
      var panes = $scope.panes = [];

      $scope.select = function(pane) {
        angular.forEach(panes, function(pane) {
          pane.selected = false;
        });
        pane.selected = true;
      }

      this.addPane = function(pane) {
        if (panes.length == 0) $scope.select(pane);
        panes.push(pane);
      }

    }],
    // Using inline template
    template:
    '<div class="tabbable">' +
      '<ul class="nav nav-tabs">' +
        '<li ng-repeat="pane in panes" ng-class="{active:pane.selected}">'+
          '<a href="" ng-click="select(pane)">{{pane.title}}</a>' +
        '</li>' +
      '</ul>' +
      '<div class="tab-content" ng-transclude></div>' +
    '</div>',
    replace: true
  };
})
.directive('pane', function() {
  return {
    require: '^customTabs',
    restrict: 'E',
    transclude: true,
    scope: { title: '@' },
```

―――――――――――――――――――――――――――――――――― Chapter 3

```
      link: function(scope, element, attrs, tabsCtrl) {
        tabsCtrl.addPane(scope);
      },
      // Using inline template
      template:
      '<div class="tab-pane" ng-class="{active: selected}"
      ng-transclude>' +
      '</div>',
      replace: true
    };
  })
```

5. Now, we will add the HTML markup to the `home.html` file:

   ```
   <!-- Custom Boostrap Tab -->
   <div style="width:600px; margin:20px auto;">
     <custom-tabs>
       <pane title="Custom Tab One">
         <div>Tab One Content.</div>
       </pane>
       <pane title="Custom Tab Two">
         <div>Tab Two Content.</div>
       </pane>
       <pane title="Custom Tab Three">
         <div>Tab Three Content.</div>
       </pane>
     </custom-tabs>
   </div>
   ```

> Note that the `style` tag on the HTML examples is not a good practice, but we use it just to center the example code on the screen. Please don't do that in production, keep your CSS files in separated files.

How it works...

In large-scale applications, it is very common to use dynamic content to populate the interface components. Our first example demonstrates how easy it is to use this type of content, by implementing a simple Bootstrap tab directive as the following code:

```
<div ng-controller="BootstrapTabCtrl">
  <tabset>
    <tab ng-repeat="tab in tabs" heading="{{tab.title}}"
    active="tab.active" disabled="tab.disabled">
```

49

Customizing and Using Bootstrap UI Directives

```
      {{tab.content}}
    </tab>
  </tabset>
</div>
```

The `$http.get ()` method makes a call to an external file, in this case the `tab-content.json` file, to load the tab contents of the directive.

```
$http.get('app/home/tab-content.json').
  success(function(data) {
    // Get dynamic data from JSON file
    $scope.tabs = data;

}).
  error(function(status) {
    // if error, show status
    console.log(status);
});
```

In the second example, we created a directive and used an inline template with the inline controller.

```
.directive('customTabs', function() {
  return {
    restrict: 'E',
    transclude: true,
    scope: {},
    controller: [ "$scope", function($scope) {
      var panes = $scope.panes = [];

      $scope.select = function(pane) {
        angular.forEach(panes, function(pane) {
          pane.selected = false;
        });
        pane.selected = true;
      }

      this.addPane = function(pane) {
        if (panes.length == 0) $scope.select(pane);
          panes.push(pane);
      }

    }],
    // Using inline template
    template:
```

```
            '<div class="tabbable">' +
            '<ul class="nav nav-tabs">' +
              '<li ng-repeat="pane in panes" ng-
              class="{active:pane.selected}">'+
              '<a href="" ng-click="select(pane)">{{pane.title}}</a>' +
              '</li>' +
            '</ul>' +
            '<div class="tab-content" ng-transclude></div>' +
            '</div>',
            replace: true
        };
    })
```

Note that this directive comprises two parts: the first simulates the links behavior as tabs, and the second activates the selected panel:

```
    .directive('pane', function() {
      return {
        require: '^customTabs',
        restrict: 'E',
        transclude: true,
        scope: { title: '@' },
        link: function(scope, element, attrs, tabsCtrl) {
          tabsCtrl.addPane(scope);
        },
        // Using inline template
        template:
        '<div class="tab-pane" ng-class="{active: selected}" ng-
        transclude>' +
        '</div>',
        replace: true
      };
    })
```

It is very common for a directive to be composed of one or more parts. A directive, in this case, depends on the operation of the other. They remain connected using the `link` property:

```
    link: function(scope, element, attrs, tabsCtrl) {
      tabsCtrl.addPane(scope);
    },
```

Customizing and Using Bootstrap UI Directives

There's more...

We can combine both examples to load external content easily using a controller and an external template in the second example, as performed in the previous examples:

```
.directive('customTabs', function() {
  return {
    restrict: 'E',
    transclude: true,
    // Declaring scope: {} we using the isolate scope and we can
    use the directive many times in the same page
    scope: {},
    controller: customCtrl.js,
    // Using external template
    template:app/common/tabs-custom-tpl.html,
    replace: true
  };
})
```

See also

- You can find more about dynamic content in the last example of this chapter. You can also check the AngularJS UI Bootstrap documentation at https://github.com/angular-ui/bootstrap/wiki

The isolate $scope

The isolate scope is a key part in building custom directives; the understanding of this topic is crucial in understanding how the scope behaves between the controller and the directive.

Remember that scope inherits from the parent scope by default. This means the controller in our case, so to avoid this default behavior we need to use the isolate scope technique.

It's pretty important to avoid accidentally read or write properties in the parent scope; let's see an example.

Getting ready

We will use our latest code from the `customTabs` directive as a starting point to illustrate the isolate scope.

Chapter 3

How to do it...

1. Let's take a look at the following highlighted code from the `customTabs` directive; focus on the `scope` property:

```
.directive('pane', function() {
  return {
    require: '^customTabs',
    restrict: 'E',
    transclude: true,
    scope: { title: '@' },
    link: function(scope, element, attrs, tabsCtrl) {
      tabsCtrl.addPane(scope);
    },
    // Using inline template
    template:
    '<div class="tab-pane" ng-class="{active: selected}" ng-transclude>' +
    '</div>',
    replace: true
  };
})
```

How it works...

The preceding block of code has a highlighted line with the following code:

```
scope: { title: '@'}
```

The isolate scope does not prototypically inherit from the parent scope (our `customTabs` directive has its own scope), but we declared the property as an empty object:

```
// Declaring scope: {} we use the isolate scope and we can use the
directive many times in the same page
scope: {},
```

We can interact with the isolate scope in three different ways:

- Attribute
- Bindings
- Expressions

Let's take a look at each of these ways.

53

Customizing and Using Bootstrap UI Directives

Attribute

Use the `@` | `@attr` signal and set one-way data binding from the parent scope to the isolate scope.

Bindings

Use the `=` | `=attr` signal, which works almost exactly like the previous example.

Expressions

Use the `&` | `&attr` signal, which serves as a wrapper to whatever we defined in Directive Definition Object.

There's more...

You can use any combination of the scope on your own directives, like the following example from Bootstrap's built-in tab directive.

The scope object, in this case, has four properties to handle `Select` and `Deselect`, tabs to show and hide the content, a property `active` to handle CSS `active` state, and a `heading` property where we can define our own heading for the tabs.

```
.directive('tab', ['$parse', function($parse) {
  return {
    require: '^tabset',
    restrict: 'EA',
    replace: true,
    templateUrl: 'template/tabs/tab.html',
    transclude: true,
    scope: {
      active: '=?',
      heading: '@',
      onSelect: '&select', //This callback is called in
      contentHeadingTransclude
      //once it inserts the tab's content into the dom
      onDeselect: '&deselect'
    },
    controller: function() {
      //Empty controller so other directives can require being
      'under' a tab
    },
    compile: function(elm, attrs, transclude) {
```

```
      return function postLink(scope, elm, attrs, tabsetCtrl) {
        scope.$watch('active', function(active) {
          if (active) {
            tabsetCtrl.select(scope);
          }
        });

        scope.disabled = false;
        if ( attrs.disabled ) {
          scope.$parent.$watch($parse(attrs.disabled),
          function(value) {
            scope.disabled = !! value;
          });
        }

        scope.select = function() {
          if ( !scope.disabled ) {
            scope.active = true;
          }
        };

        tabsetCtrl.addTab(scope);
        scope.$on('$destroy', function() {
          tabsetCtrl.removeTab(scope);
        });

        //We need to transclude later, once the content container
        is ready.
        //when this link happens, we're inside a tab heading.
        scope.$transcludeFn = transclude;
      };
    }
  };
}])
```

See also

- You can find more about isolate scopes on the $compile API at https://docs.angularjs.org/api/ng/service/$compile

Building accordion tab directives

Another way to deal with Bootstrap UI directives is to override the default HTML template. This can be done in two ways: inside the HTML file or externally.

As you may have observed, Angular Bootstrap has two files: one called `ui-bootstrap-tpls.js` and the other just `ui-bootstrap.js`.

The difference is simple, the `tpls` suffix at the end of the filename indicates that the file has all the Bootstrap templates inside, and the others don't.

If you try to use the `ui-bootstrap.js` file you will receive an error because the compiled code doesn't find the templates, and you must provide templates for all the widgets.

Perhaps this is not a good idea when you want to override one or two components, so consider using a custom build. The following technique will be very helpful.

> You can create your own custom build for UI bootstrap and pick only the components you need at http://angular-ui.github.io/bootstrap/#/getting_started.

Getting ready

We will still use the same code base for this recipe, but this time, we will use a different CSS file to style the accordion tabs and override the default template using another template in the same file.

How to do it...

1. Let's add the following CSS file; we saved the file in `app/assets/` in the root application folder:

   ```
   .accordion-panel {
     bottom: 20px;
     background-color: #3193A9;
     border: 1px solid #ccc;
     color: #fff;
     margin: 10px auto;
   }
   .accordion-body {
     padding: 15px;
     border-top:1px solid #ccc;
     background-color: #fff;
   ```

```css
    color: #000;
}
.accordion-heading {
  padding: 10px 15px;
  border-bottom: 1px solid transparent;
}
.accordion-heading > .dropdown .dropdown-toggle {
  color: inherit;
}
.accordion-title {
  margin-top: 0;
  margin-bottom: 0;
  font-size: 16px;
  color: inherit;
}
.accordion-title > a {
  color: inherit;
  text-decoration: none;
  cursor: pointer;
  font-weight: 100;
}
```

2. Note that we are using different class names from the original Bootstrap template. Now, append the following controller to the `homeCtrl` file, as shown in the previous examples:

   ```js
   .controller('AccordionCtrl', function ($scope) {

     // Add some content to accordion
     $scope.groups = [
       {
         title: 'Header Content One',
         content: 'Body Content One'
       },
       {
         title: 'Header Content Two',
           content: 'Body Content Two'
       },
       {
         title: 'Header Content Three',
         content: 'Body Content Three'
       }
     ];

   });
   ```

Customizing and Using Bootstrap UI Directives

3. The controller is pretty simple and only has an array with some sample content. Add the following code to the `home.html` file, right after the custom tabs:

```html
<!-- Bootstrap Accordion -->
<div style="width:600px; margin:20px auto;">
  <div ng-controller="AccordionCtrl">
    <accordion close-others="oneAtATime">
      <accordion-group heading="{{group.title}}" ng-repeat="group in groups">
      {{group.content}}
      </accordion-group>
    </accordion>
  </div>
</div>
<!-- Overhide the default bootstrap template -->
<script type="text/ng-template"
id="template/accordion/accordion-group.html">
  <div class="accordion-group">
    <div class="accordion-panel">
      <div class="accordion-heading">
        <h4 class="accordion-title">
          <a class="accordion-toggle" ng-click="isOpen =
          !isOpen" accordion-transclude="heading">
          {{heading}}
          </a>
        </h4>
      </div>
      <div class="accordion-body" collapse="!isOpen">
        <div class="accordion-inner" ng-transclude></div>
      </div>
    </div>
  </div>
</script>
```

The result will be similar to the following screenshot:

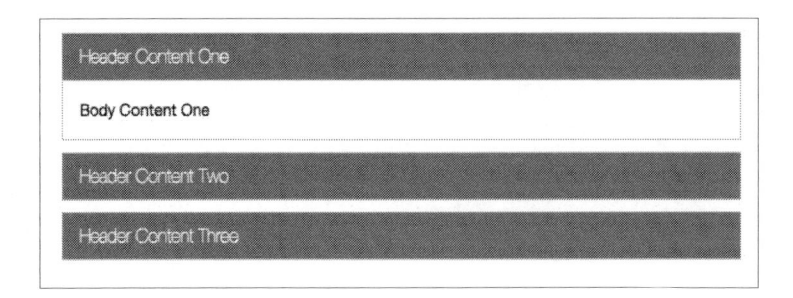

How it works...

The code inside the `AccordionCtrl` controller is pretty simple. We have just added some text to create the headers and content, but we have kept the default HTML markup:

```
<div ng-controller="AccordionCtrl">
  <accordion close-others="oneAtATime">
    <accordion-group heading="{{group.title}}" ng-repeat="group in
    groups">
    {{group.content}}
    </accordion-group>
  </accordion>
</div>
```

The magic happens right in the script template, below the `accordion` tags:

```
<script type="text/ng-template" id="template/accordion/accordion-
group.html">
  <div class="accordion-group">
    <div class="accordion-panel">
      <div class="accordion-heading">
        <h4 class="accordion-title">
          <a class="accordion-toggle" ng-click="isOpen = !isOpen"
          accordion-transclude="heading">
          {{heading}}
          </a>
        </h4>
      </div>
      <div class="accordion-body" collapse="!isOpen">
        <div class="accordion-inner" ng-transclude></div>
      </div>
    </div>
  </div>
</script>
```

The template ID keeps the default Bootstrap path to the inline templates, but the content has been entirely rewritten using the CSS classes created at the beginning of the recipe.

Customizing and Using Bootstrap UI Directives

There's more...

We can create any type of template and still use the default directive markup.

Without our template, the default directive will look like this:

| Header Content One |
| Body Content One |
| Header Content Two |
| Header Content Three |

> It is always helpful to inspect the code of Bootstrap directives to understand how things work, as the entire file has comments and examples of using directives in the markup of HTML.

Loading dynamic content

As we have previously commented, loading dynamic content in web applications is very common. In this recipe, we will see how to connect to the public GitHub API to show repositories from a particular user.

Getting ready

We will continue to keep the same base code of the previous examples, including the latter with our custom accordion.

How to do it...

1. Add the following code to the `home.html` file, right after the last accordion:

    ```html
    <!-- Bootstrap Accordion loading Dynamic Content -->
    <div style="width:600px; margin:20px auto;">
      <div ng-controller="AccordionCtrlDynamic">
        <accordion close-others="oneAtATime">
          <accordion-group heading="{{repo.name}} - Stars: {{repo.stargazers_count}}" ng-repeat="repo in repos">
            {{repo.description}}
    ```

Chapter 3

```
        </accordion-group>
      </accordion>
    </div>
  </div>
```

2. Now, append the new controller to the end of the `homeCtrl.js` file:

    ```
    .controller('AccordionCtrlDynamic', function ($scope, $http) {

      // Add some content to accordion
      $http.get('https://api.github.com/users/twbs/repos').
      success(function(data) {
        // Get dynamic data from JSON file
        $scope.repos = data;
      }).
      error(function(status) {
        // if error, show status
        console.log(status);
      });

    });
    ```

How it works...

Note that we are using the `$http.get()` method again, because GitHub offers a public API for the developer and we can access it without any special key or token:

```
$http.get('https://api.github.com/users/twbs/repos')
```

The user, in this case, is the Twitter Bootstrap Repository.

As we have kept the same custom directive, our layout remains the same as the previous example, but here, we have also retrieved the repository name, the amount of stars, and inside, a description about the repo.

```
<accordion-group heading="{{repo.name}} - Stars: {{repo.stargazers_count}}" ng-repeat="repo in repos">
  {{repo.description}}
</accordion-group>
```

Customizing and Using Bootstrap UI Directives

The result is similar to the following screenshot:

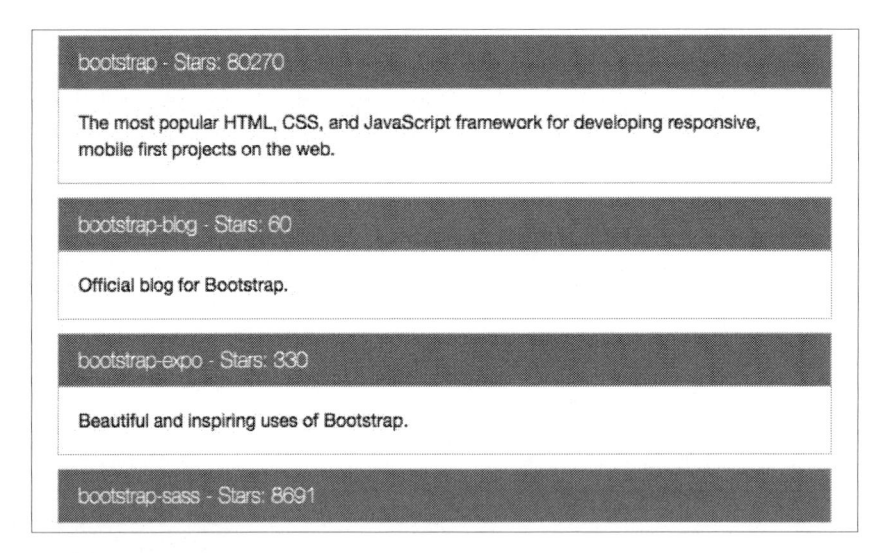

bootstrap - Stars: 80270

The most popular HTML, CSS, and JavaScript framework for developing responsive, mobile first projects on the web.

bootstrap-blog - Stars: 60

Official blog for Bootstrap.

bootstrap-expo - Stars: 330

Beautiful and inspiring uses of Bootstrap.

bootstrap-sass - Stars: 8691

There's more...

We can combine different interface components using the directives of this chapter and easily build a small application showing some GitHub data.

For instance, we can extend the previous example and use an input model to bind the username and make a dynamic search for users:

```
<input type="text" ng-model="userName"/>

$http.get('https://api.github.com/users/userName/repos')
```

4
Creating Interactive jQuery UI Directives

In this chapter, we will cover:

- A simple directive example
- Manipulating the DOM with jQuery
- The compile and link functions
- Creating the jQuery UI draggable directive
- Creating the jQuery UI droppable directive

Introduction

Some time ago, jQuery revolutionized web development. It provided a simple way to manipulate the DOM, created intuitive abstractions for common operations, and created a single API that could be used across many different web browsers.

However, nowadays some frameworks have a very specific way of manipulating HTML content, such as AngularJS.

But as we mentioned before, using jQuery in AngularJS applications cannot be that simple. In this chapter, you will see how to create some directives and use the jQuery interface components, specifically the jQuery UI.

Creating Interactive jQuery UI Directives

A simple directive example

AngularJS has its own version of jQuery, known as jQuery Lite. This version has just over 30 methods, some of them a little limited, as is the case with `find()`, `parent()`, and `on()`, among others. AngularJS added some extra methods to the jQuery Lite version such as `$destroy()`, `injector()`, and `inheritedData()`, which is the same as `$data()`. Along with many others.

Another important thing to note is that the $ dollar sign has no effect here. The AngularJS equivalent is `angular.element`, so something like this:

```
angular.element() === jQuery() === $()
```

In most cases, it is sufficient to use the built-in version of jQuery on AngularJS; however, if you require any method that is not listed in the official documentation, you can include the full version of jQuery in your HTML file, always put before the AngularJS script.

Getting ready

In this chapter, we will also use the generator-angm, as we did in the previous chapter.

This time we will call our application `jquerydirectives`. We will follow the same pattern as the previous chapter and add directives and example code that we will use in the next recipes.

How to do it...

1. Create a new directory and name it `jquery-ui-directives`.
2. Open your terminal window, go to the project folder and type:

    yo angm

3. Add the following code to `homeCtrl.js` and append it to `HomeCtrl`:

    ```
    .controller('DateCtrl', function($scope) {
      $scope.date = new Date();
    });
    ```

4. Now let's add the directive code and append it to `DateCtrl`:

    ```
    .directive('datepicker', function() {
      return {
        restrict: 'A',
        require : 'ngModel',
        link : function (scope, elem, attrs, ngModelCtrl) {
          elem.datepicker({
            dateFormat:'dd/mm/yy',
            onSelect: function (date) {
    ```

```
                ngModelCtrl.$setViewValue(date);
                scope.$apply();
            }
        });
    }
  }
});
```

5. Finally, we add the following HTML code to the `home.html` file, then the jQuery UI script tag at the end of all scripts, and then the CSS link before all CSS:

```
<link rel="stylesheet"
href="https://code.jquery.com/ui/1.11.4/themes/cupertino/jquery-
ui.css">
<script src="https://code.jquery.com/ui/1.11.4/jquery-
ui.min.js"></script>
<div ng-controller="DateCtrl">
  <h1> Date: {{date | date:"dd/MM/yyyy"}}</h1>
  <input type="text" ng-model="date" datepicker />
</div>
```

> Note that it is very important to add the script and CSS tag before the `<!-- injector:xx -->` comments tag.

Here is the result using the cupertino theme from jQuery UI:

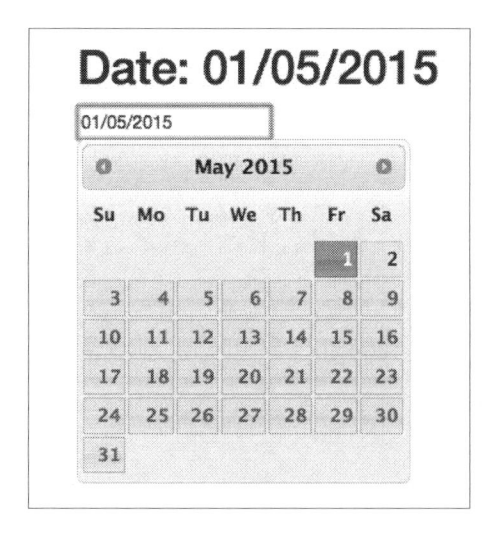

Creating Interactive jQuery UI Directives

How it works...

In the following code snippet, you'll see that we restricted the directive to an attribute (restrict: 'A'), used the Link() function to manipulate the DOM, and initiates the datepicker from jQuery UI using the elem parameter. This is similar to $('#someHTMLelement').datepicker():

```
link : function (scope, elem, attrs, ngModelCtrl) {
  elem.datepicker({
    dateFormat:'dd/mm/yy',
    onSelect: function (date) {
      ngModelCtrl.$setViewValue(date);
      scope.$apply();
    }
  });
}
```

We used the scope.$apply() method to update the DOM with the new value.

There's more...

We made use of ngModelCtrl as the fourth parameter for the link(scope, elem, attrs, ngModelCtrl) function to update the model $scope.date on DateCtrl.

See also

- You can find more about ngModelCtrl in the official AngularJS documentation at https://docs.angularjs.org/api/ng/type/ngModel.NgModelController

Manipulating the DOM with jQuery

Another simple example of manipulating the DOM using jQuery is to build a simple resizable component, called resizebox here, analogous to the resizable() method from the jQuery UI. Note that this example only has a demonstrative effect.

Chapter 4

Getting ready

We will use the same code as in the previous example, since we already have our AngularJS application configured and running. Don't forget to keep the CSS and JS links to jQuery UI in the `index.html` file:

```
<link rel="stylesheet"
href="https://code.jquery.com/ui/1.11.4/themes/cupertino/jquery-
ui.css">
<script src="https://code.jquery.com/ui/1.11.4/jquery-
ui.min.js"></script>
```

How to do it...

1. Let's add the directive code right after the `datepicker` directive in the `homeCtrl.js` file. Remember, we're still using the same code example for this chapter:

   ```
   .directive('resizebox', function () {

     return {
       restrict: 'A',
       scope: {},
       link: function postLink(scope, elem, attrs) {
         elem.resizable();
       }
     };
   });
   ```

2. As we are dealing with a simple DOM manipulation, we don't need a controller for this example, we just need the HTML code to use the directive. So let's add the HTML code to the `home.html` file:

   ```
   <div resizebox class="box">Content: jQuery Resize</div>
   ```

3. Before we see the final result, we need to add some CSS styling with a border and background color. Let's do it:

   ```
   <style>
   .box {
     /*Set min-width to avoid text shrink*/
     min-width: 300px;
     height: 200px;
     border: 1px solid #444;
     color: #000;
   ```

Creating Interactive jQuery UI Directives

```
        text-align: center;
        background-color: #ccc;
    }
    </style>
```

You can add the CSS in `home.html` inside the `style` tags on the first line of the file, just for this example.

How it works...

The operation is very simple; since we don't need to manipulate any information within our div resizable, our directive consists of the minimum necessary to boot it.

We made use of the `postLink()` function to notify the DOM that the element was loaded, similar to `$(document).ready();` from jQuery.

The `elem.resizable();` here is similar to `$('element').resizable();`.

There's more...

The `postLink` function can be used with the `compile` function, such as in the following example:

```
compile: function compile(tElement, tAttrs, transclude) {
    return {
        pre: function preLink(scope, iElement, iAttrs, controller) {
        ... },
        post: function postLink(scope, iElement, iAttrs, controller) {
        ... }
    }
    // or
    // return function postLink( ... ) { ... }
},
```

The compile and link functions

Another point that generates a lot of confusion is the `compile` and `link` functions. In previous chapters, you saw how the `link` function was utilized; however, we will take a different, didactic approach in this recipe.

Getting ready

We will continue to use our sample application, and we will add a directive to create a progress bar component.

How to do it...

1. Let's add the following code to the end of the `homeCtrl.js` file and append it to the `resizebox` directive:

    ```
    .directive('progressbar', function () {

      return {
        restrict: 'A',
        scope: {
          progress: '=progressbar'
        },
        // link: function postLink(scope, elem, attrs) {
        //   elem.progressbar({
        //     value: scope.progress
        //   });
        // },
        compile: function () {
          return function (scope, elem) {
            elem.progressbar({
              value: scope.progress
            });
          };
        }
      };
    })
    ```

2. Right after the directive code, let's add the controller code:

    ```
    .controller('progressbarCtrl', function ($scope) {
      // Set a value to the progressbar
      $scope.value = 30
    });
    ```

Creating Interactive jQuery UI Directives

The expected result is similar to the following picture: a progress bar partially filled:

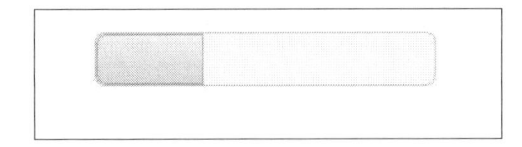

Note that we are still using the same jQuery UI theme.

How it works...

Although the preceding example is basic, it is very useful to help you understand the `compile()` function. First, let's check what the official documentation says:

> *Compiler is an Angular service which traverses the DOM looking for attributes. The compilation process happens in two phases.*
>
> *Compile: traverse the DOM and collect all of the directives. The result is a linking function.*
>
> *Link: combine the directives with a scope and produce a live view. Any changes in the scope model are reflected in the view, and any user interactions with the view are reflected in the scope model. This makes the scope model the single source of truth.*

We used the compile function instead of the `link()` function to accomplish the same goal of showing the progress bar, as we can see here:

```
compile: function () {
  return function (scope, elem) {
    elem.progressbar({
      value: scope.progress
    });
  };
}
```

We can perform the same task using the `link()` function, but for performance reasons we used the `compile()` function. The main difference is:

- The `link()` function attaches event listeners to the HTML template, and starts after the `compile()` function
- The `compile()` function manipulates the DOM of the HTML template and the directive also has a chance of modifying the DOM node before the use of scope

There's more...

When we create our directives, we can use any combination of functions, such as: `link()`, `compile()`, `template()`, `controller()`, and many others, including more than one at a time. As we commented in previous chapters, customized directives are very flexible.

See also

- You can find out more about compiler at `https://code.angularjs.org/1.2.26/docs/guide/compiler#compiler`

Creating the jQuery UI draggable directive

In the jQuery world, simple interface components such as draggable are easily built, as jQuery UI provides us with all the necessary plugins to accomplish this task. In an AngularJS application, easy things must follow some steps, in this case custom directives.

Getting ready

We are still using the same code base as in the previous example.

How to do it...

1. Let's append the `draggable` directive code to the `homeCtrl.js` file, right after the `progressbar` controller:

   ```
   .directive('draggable', function () {
     return {
       restrict: 'A',
       scope: {},
       link: function (scope, elem, attrs) {
         elem.draggable({
         revert: "invalid",
         });
       }
     };
   });
   ```

2. Now, add the directive HTML code to `home.html` file, right after the `progressbar` div:

   ```
   <div class="drag ui-widget-content" draggable>
     <p>Draggable Content</p>
   </div>
   ```

Creating Interactive jQuery UI Directives

How it works...

As you saw in the previous examples, we are manipulating the DOM of our AngularJS application using the jQuery UI interface components.

> You do not have to reinvent the wheel unless you really need to.

This is an effective way to build rich, interactive interfaces using what we already have on hand, in this case, all the jQuery UI components.

We created the directive as an attribute, and it can be applied to any user interface element:

```
restrict: 'A',
```

We used the isolated scope with: `scope:{}` and the `link` function to instantiate the element with the `.draggable()` jQuery function.

As we are using the jQuery UI scripts, we have all the `draggable` methods available to us inside the `elem.draggable()` function.

On the HTML side, we applied the jQuery UI style using the `ui-widget-content` class.

There's more...

Also, we can use any jQuery method inside the directive such as `destroy`, `disable`, `enable`, `instance`, `option`, and `widget`.

See also

- You can find out more about the methods and events from draggable components at https://api.jqueryui.com/draggable/

Chapter 4

Creating the jQuery UI droppable directive

As we saw in the previous example, a draggable component may be more useful using another component known as a droppable. We'll look at a way to practice combining them.

The final result will be similar to the following images:

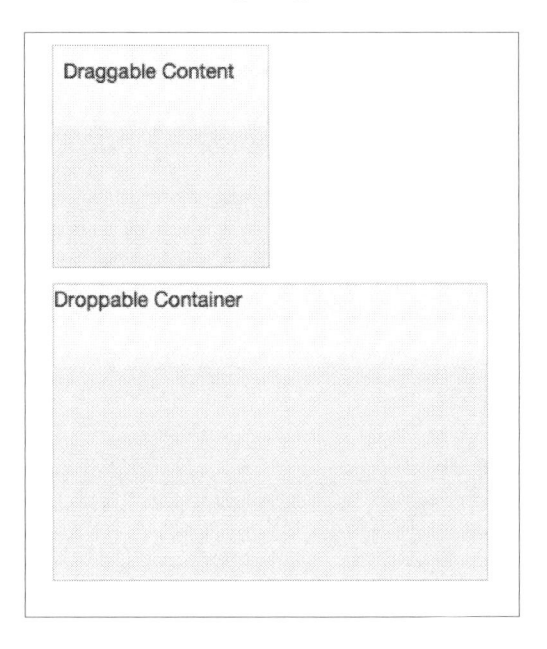

Now the draggable and droppable combined:

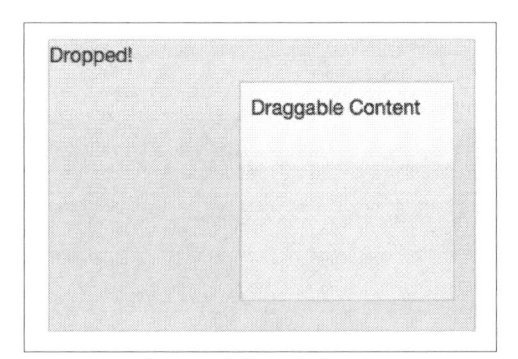

Creating Interactive jQuery UI Directives

Getting ready

We are using the same code base as in the previous example.

How to do it...

1. Add the following code to the `homeCtrl.js` file, right after the `draggable` directive:

```
.directive('droppable', function () {
  return {
    restrict: 'A',
    scope: {},
      link: function (scope, elem, attrs) {
        elem.droppable({
          activeClass: "ui-state-default",
          hoverClass: "ui-state-hover",
          drop:function(event,ui) {
            $(this).addClass( "ui-state-highlight" )
            .find( "p" )
            .html( "Dropped!" );
          }
        });
      }
  };
});
```

2. Add the following HTML content to the `home.html` file, right after the draggable content:

```
<div class="drop ui-widget-content" droppable>
  <p>Droppable Container</p>
</div>
```

How it works...

So, we're still using the attribute directive `restrict: 'A'`, and we can apply it to any HTML element.

The `link()` function instantiates the droppable component, as in the previous example for the draggable component.

In this example, we have a function called `drop()`. The behavior here is very simple: we just applied a CSS class to the droppable element when it received a droppable element.

There's more...

Also, we can use any jQuery method inside the directive, such as `destroy`, `disable`, `enable`, `instance`, `option`, and `widget`.

See also

- You can find out more about the methods and events of draggable components at `https://api.jqueryui.com/droppable/`

5
Implementing Custom Directives with Yeoman Generators

In this chapter, we will cover:

- Creating the baseline app with generator-angm
- Generator best practices
- How to implement the ngMap directive
- Using the Angular-Loading-Bar directive
- Implementing the ng-Grid directive

Introduction

Every web application has a similar folder structure and common components. Before beginning the development itself, we need to think of the whole structure and create a lot of boilerplate code each time for all the applications.

As I have mentioned in previous chapters, code generators can facilitate our task. In this chapter, we will see how to make the most of a generator and integrate some directives in a ready-made structure.

Implementing Custom Directives with Yeoman Generators

Creating the baseline app with generator-angm

We have many options for Yeoman generators; each has its own peculiarities and serves very well for one or more tasks and types of applications.

In the following example, we will continue using the ANGM generator (the same from the previous chapters), which while writing this book has received some updates that will further facilitate the development of modular AngularJS applications.

Getting ready

The first step for the next recipes is to update the generator that we were already using. To do so, open your terminal window and type the following command:

`npm install -g generator-angm`

> You can get more information and learn more about generator-angm on the official site: `http://newaeonweb.com.br/generator-angm/`.

Now, let's start to create the baseline itself.

How to do it...

1. On the terminal window, use the following command:

   `yo angm`

2. The generator will ask for the application name, so type the following command:

   `yeomananddirectives`

3. This is the fun part. The generator will create all necessary directories and files for an application with AngularJS. Let's check the result on the terminal window and type:

   `grunt dev`

   After this command, your default browser will open and you'd be able to see the generator's welcome screen.

How it works...

The two previous commands do all the heavy lifting of creating the necessary baseline for any web application with AngularJS.

At the final stage of the generator code, we see the following files added to the project:

```
bower install    es5-shim#3.1.0
bower install    angular#1.4.0
bower install    angular-resource#1.4.0
bower install    bootstrap#3.3.4
bower install    angular-sanitize#1.4.0
bower install    angular-mocks#1.4.0
bower install    angular-ui-router#0.2.15
bower install    angular-bootstrap#0.11.2
bower install    angular-route#1.4.0
bower install    angular-animate#1.4.0
bower install    angular-cookies#1.4.0
bower install    json3#3.3.1
bower install    angular-touch#1.4.0
bower install    jquery#2.1.4
```

Generator installed dependencies

This is because the generator already includes all the dependencies necessary for a web project. We can see that it uses the latest versions of AngularJS and some dependent libraries as `bootstrap`.

As you can see in step 3, the generator already included the `Grunt.JS` task manager.

There's more...

The generator we've used also benefits us in many other ways. It has subgenerators that save work when it comes to the creation of filters, controllers, routes, and directives.

See also

To facilitate the development, we can use the `grunt build` command, which prepares our application to be put into production.

In addition, we can test our application using Karma, a JavaScript test runner. Open the terminal and type the following command:

npm test

Implementing Custom Directives with Yeoman Generators

As part of the generator, all test structures are automatically created. By starting it, we can write all the necessary tests for our application.

Generator best practices

When we use a tool for the solution of a specific problem, it is very common to worry about the best practices of the market for utilization of such a tool.

It happens frequently, and AngularJS is no different. Due to the large amount of tools, generators, and boilerplates, there is a common lookout on what best fits our application. Depending on the choice, this can become a nightmare in the long run, and your code will become a mess.

Since the goal of this book is not to discuss the best practices for development with AngularJS, we will stick to best practices for Directives AngularJS and this particular generator.

Getting ready

We will use the code generated in the previous recipe to identify some relevant points for the implementation of directives.

How to do it...

1. In your favorite editor, open the application we just created in the previous example.
2. It is possible to visualize the entire structure of directories and files created by the generator, as we can see in the following screenshot:

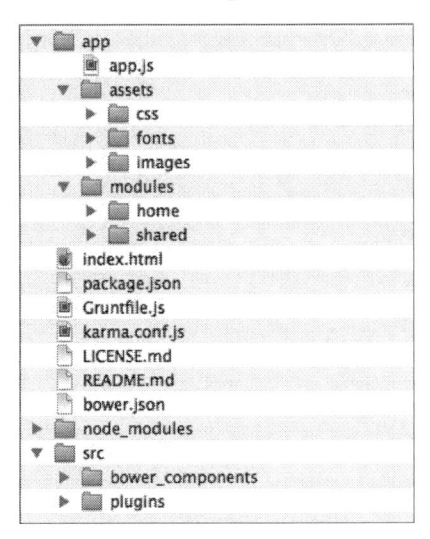

Application directory structure

How it works...

As we mentioned earlier, we are using a generator that organizes our code by feature, that is, the application will be distributed by modules.

The `modules` folder stores all the modules of the application; we will see a clearer example of this in the next recipe.

The other folders are self explanatory, but the main advantage in the utilization of the generator is that we do not create any folders and files at this first stage.

In addition, we can see that there is a `shared` folder within the `modules` folder. This folder can store all custom directives that we will create in an AngularJS application. Finally, we also have the `home` folder, which is a built-in module created by the generator.

The `bower_components` folder stores all the libraries used by AngularJS and can even store future installations that are necessary for the project.

Some directives can be installed through Bower, and the generator-angm will add them to the `index.html` page by just running the `grunt dev` command.

There's more...

Let's add a new module to the application to see how the generator works with subgenerators.

On the terminal window, just type the following command:

`yo angm:angm-module`

Just like the previous recipe, we need to insert a name for the new module: `mapping`. After the generator has finished the job, we will have the following files created:

```
? What would you like to call the module? mapping
? Which files would you like your module to include? Controller, Route, View (HTML), Service
   create app/modules/mapping/mappingCtrl.js
   create app/modules/mapping/mappingRoute.js
   create app/modules/mapping/mapping.html
   create app/modules/mapping/mappingService.js
   create app/modules/mapping/mapping-test.js
```

Now, we just need to run the `grunt dev` command and the module can be accessed through the URL `http://127.0.0.1:8000/#!/mapping`.

Implementing Custom Directives with Yeoman Generators

How to implement the ngMap directive

In the following recipe, we'll see how to install a directive into an AngularJS application using the Bower dependency manager. Throughout our book, there are several alternatives to create and customize directives; we can use third-party directives.

In the next example, we'll use the `ng-map` directive. As the name says, it is a directive for creating and manipulating maps.

> You can find more information on ng-map at `http://ngmap.github.io/`.

Getting ready

We will use the same code that we used in the previous example as a starting point. In addition, it is recommended that you already have Bower installed on your system. If you don't have or know Bower, don't worry, we will demonstrate how to install it manually.

How to do it...

1. At the root project folder, open your terminal window and type:

    `bower install ngmap --save`

2. To get the directive to work properly, you need to add the Google Maps script. In this example, we will use the code directly from the Google CDN through this link: `//maps.google.com/maps/api/js`.

3. Open the `index.html` file and add the following script tag right after the `mappingService.js` script:

    ```
    <script src="//maps.google.com/maps/api/js"></script>
    ```

4. Add the `ng-map` script right after the Google Maps script:

    ```
    <script src="src/bower_components/ngmap/build/scripts/ng-map.min.js"></script>
    ```

> Don't place any code inside the `<!-- injector:js --><!-- endinjector-->` tag; when generators run any task, this block of code is always replaced.

5. Open the `app.js` file and add the following highlighted code to the AngularJS dependencies:

```
angular.module('yeomananddirectives', [
  'ngResource',
  'ui.bootstrap',
  'ngCookies',
  'ngAnimate',
  'ngTouch',
  'ngSanitize',
  'ui.router',
  'mapping',
  'ngMap',
])
```

6. At this point, we have our directive maps installed in our application. Now, let's see the necessary steps to use the directive. Open `mapping.html` and add the following code:

```
<map center="-23.630153, -46.563964" zoom="13">
  <div ng-repeat="pos in positions">
  <marker position="{{pos.lat}},{{pos.lng}}"
  animation="DROP"></marker>
  </div>
</map>
```

7. Open `mappingCtrl.js` and add the following code:

```
var positions = [
  { lat: -23.630153, lng: -46.563964 },
  { lat: -23.625828, lng: -46.571946 },
  { lat: -23.634006, lng: -46.576066 },
  { lat: -23.624883 ,lng: -46.564209 }
];
$scope.positions = positions;
```

8. Let's check the final result. Open your terminal window and type the following command:

   grunt dev

Your default browser will open at the application welcome screen. Check the mapping URL `http://127.0.0.1:8000/#!/mapping`.

Implementing Custom Directives with Yeoman Generators

How it works...

Let's understand what we've done with the previous commands. One of the functionalities of the generator we are using is to keep all the application code organized. With the `bower install` command, the new directive was added as a component in the `bower_components` folder within the directory `src`.

This is a common practice when dealing with `bower`. You may notice that we have a file called `.bower` at the root of our project. This is where we determine the place to install all frontend components managed by `bower`. The `--save` option at the end of the command saves the module name and the version in the `bower.json` file.

The next steps are pretty simple. We add the scripts from `ngmap` to the `index.html` file, and add `ngMap` as a dependency on `angular.module('yeomananddirectives', ['ngMap']);`.

We then use a very basic combination of features from the `ng-map` directive, `<map center="-23.630153, -46.563964" zoom="13">`, just to center the map on the screen and set the zoom.

Inside the `ng-map` directive, we use the ng-repeat to generate some markers with `ng-repeat="pos in positions"`. Finally, in our controller, we set some coordinate points, showing the flexibility of `ng-map`.

There's more...

We can use a service to load the positions and then add to map. Let's see how to do it.

Add the following code to the `mappingService.js` file inside the `mapping` module:

```
var positions = [
  { lat: -23.630153, lng: -46.563964 },
  { lat: -23.625828, lng: -46.571946 },
  { lat: -23.634006, lng: -46.576066 },
  { lat: -23.624883 ,lng: -46.564209 }
];

return {
  all: function() {
    return positions;
  }
}
```

Chapter 5

Now, add the `mappingService` factory to `mappingCtrl` as a dependency:

```
angular.module('mapping')
.controller('MappingCtrl', ['$scope','MappingService', function
($scope, MappingService) {

  // Using a service
  $scope.positions = MappingService.all();

}]);
```

In this way, we have a greater flexibility to use this directive.

> Note that our service in a real application will be an endpoint to a server that returns the positions stored in a database.

See also

- You can find more information at `https://github.com/allenhwkim/angularjs-google-maps`

Using the Angular-Loading-Bar directive

In interactive applications, it is very common to exchange data with the database using AJAX and consuming a web service or JSON endpoint.

Often, the request may take a few seconds to return the answer (the response). Then, we need to warn our user to wait for the request to complete. For this purpose, we use a directive called angular-loading-bar.

In this recipe, we will see a different way to implement a custom directive. Let's do it manually using the generators structure.

Getting ready

First of all, we need to download the directive files from the angular-loading-bar directive at `https://github.com/chieffancypants/angular-loading-bar/tree/master/build`.

We will use the `loading-bar.min.css` and `loading-bar.min.js` files. Also, we will use the same code base that we used in the previous chapter.

Implementing Custom Directives with Yeoman Generators

How to do it...

1. Create a new directory inside the `shared` folder and name it `directives`: `app/modules/shared/directives/`.
2. Create a new directory inside the `directives` folder and name it `loading-bar`: `app/modules/shared/directives/loading-bar/`.
3. Now, place the CSS and JS files (`loading-bar.min.css` and `loading-bar.min.js`) inside the `loading-bar` folder.
4. The next step is to add the module `loading-bar` as a dependency in the `app.js` file. Place the following highlighted code:

```
angular.module('yeomananddirectives', [
    'ngResource',
    'ui.bootstrap',
    'ngCookies',
    'ngAnimate',
    'ngTouch',
    'ngSanitize',
    'ui.router',
    'mapping',
    'ngMap',
    'angular-loading-bar'
])
```

5. Finally, we need to add the CSS and JS file to the `index.html` file:

```
<link rel="stylesheet" href="/app/modules/shared/directives/loading-bar/loading-bar.min.css">
<script src="/app/modules/shared/directives/loading-bar/loading-bar.min.js"></script>
```

> Step 5 is not required when we use the Grunt task from generator-angm; the generator has a built-in feature to install and link files.

6. Now, we need to perform just one more step to check the final result. Let's add a service to load some sample data. Let's add the following content to a new blank file and save it as `locations.json` in the `assets` folder:

```
[
    { "lat": -23.630153, "lng": -46.563964 },
    { "lat": -23.625828, "lng": -46.571946 },
    { "lat": -23.634006, "lng": -46.576066 },
    { "lat": -23.624883 ,"lng": -46.564209 },
```

```
    { "lat": -23.624890 ,"lng": -46.564210 },
    { "lat": -23.634991 ,"lng": -46.574201 },
    { "lat": -23.654589 ,"lng": -46.584222 },
    { "lat": -23.674881 ,"lng": -46.594199 },
    { "lat": -23.694884 ,"lng": -46.554208 }
]
```

7. Now, let's create a new service to get these locations using the $resource AngularJS feature inside `mappingService.js`. Add the following lines:

   ```
   .factory('JsonLocations', ['$resource', function
   ($resource) {
     return $resource('app/assets/locations.json' );
   }]);
   ```

8. Go back to `mappingCtrl` and replace the following code:

   ```
   // Using a service
     //$scope.positions = MappingService.all();
     $scope.positions = JsonLocations.query();
   ```

9. Finally, add the new `JsonLocations` service to the controller:

   ```
   .controller('MappingCtrl',
   ['$scope','MappingService','JsonLocations', function
   ($scope, MappingService, JsonLocations){}
   ```

10. Open your terminal window and type the following command:

    grunt concurrent

How it works...

The directive we used intercepts the $http requests, and this includes $resource as well. It shows a loading bar on the screen accompanied by a spinner in the upper-right corner. Then, throughout the HTTP request, the `loading-bar` is automatically activated.

In this example, we implemented the directive manually, that is, we did not use the Bower dependency manager.

A special feature of generator-angm is to propose an optimized directory structure for AngularJS applications.

The `shared` folder can store all custom directives that will be used in our project. We can store all the directives in the same way, each with its own folder.

We open a parenthesis here to a relevant comment that should be in your head right now.

Implementing Custom Directives with Yeoman Generators

When we use Bower, its purpose is to facilitate managing dependencies, storing all the code (packages) in one place. It provides a series of benefits, but at times, we do not want to update all the project dependencies.

As we know, AngularJS is growing very quickly and if our project has a dozen dependencies, we need to ensure that every library evolution is compatible with our code.

A safe way to do this is by isolating some components to be shared across the application. So, we use the `shared` folder where we can manually take care of the evolution and compatibility of the used libraries.

This code example used a powerful AngularJS resource know as `$resource` to load the content that will be handled by the `ngmap` directive. Thus, we can see a good example that is very close to a real AngularJS application.

There's more...

Some steps that we used in this recipe could have been avoided if we used the generator task, since we do not need to manually enter all the scripts used in our `index.html` file.

For this, just run the following command:

```
grunt dev
```

All dependencies are added to the `index.html` file. We just need to include the `'angular-loading-bar'` directive on `app.js` and it's done.

Implementing the ng-grid directive

In this recipe, we'll see how to use an extremely useful interface component used in a large number of web applications. We're talking about `ng-grid`, a very useful custom directive to deal with dynamic tabular data.

In this example, we will use an external public API to grab some data.

Getting ready

We're still using the same code base that we used in the previous chapter. Let's add a new module.

Open your terminal window on the root project folder and type the following command:

```
yo angm:angm-module
```

Name the new module as `gridexample`. When the generator finishes its work, we will have the following result:

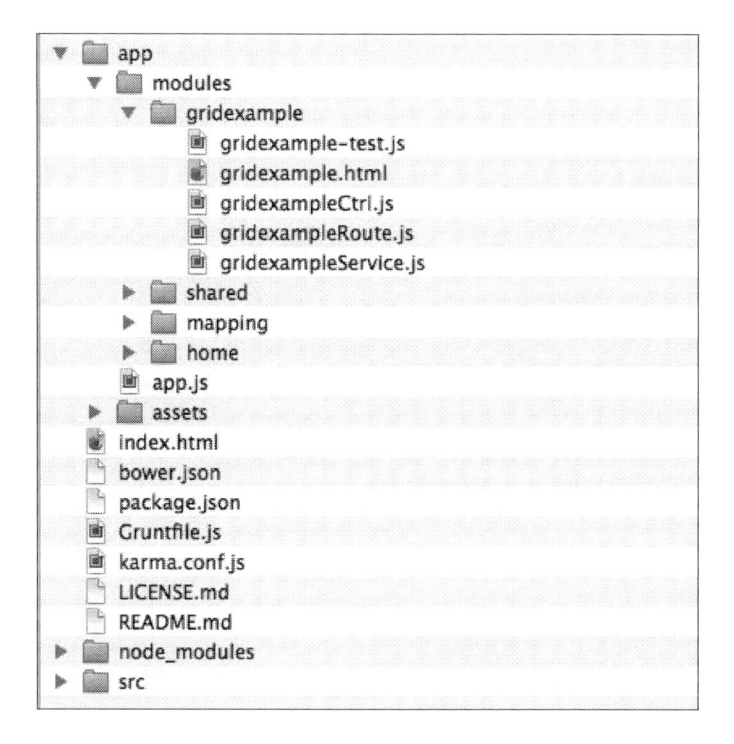

```
▼ app
    ▼ modules
        ▼ gridexample
              gridexample-test.js
              gridexample.html
              gridexampleCtrl.js
              gridexampleRoute.js
              gridexampleService.js
        ▶ shared
        ▶ mapping
        ▶ home
        app.js
    ▶ assets
    index.html
    bower.json
    package.json
    Gruntfile.js
    karma.conf.js
    LICENSE.md
    README.md
▶ node_modules
▶ src
```

The `gridexample` module was created, and we can access it with the URL `http://127.0.0.1:8000/#!/gridexample`. Now, let's see how to implement `ng-grid`.

How to do it...

1. First of all, let's create a factory to grab our data from a simple API. Add the following highlighted code to `gridexampleService.js`:

    ```
    'use strict';

    /**
     * @ngdoc function
     * @name app.service:gridexampleService
     * @description
     * # gridexampleService
     * Service of the app
     */
    ```

Implementing Custom Directives with Yeoman Generators

```
angular.module('gridexample')
.factory('GridexampleService', ['$resource', function ($resource)
{
  //return $resource('http://ontariobeerapi.ca:80/beers/');
  return $resource('app/assets/brewer.json');
}]);
```

2. Add the new service to `gridexampleCtrl.js`:

```
angular.module('gridexample')
.controller('GridexampleCtrl', ['$scope', 'GridexampleService',
function ($scope, GridexampleService) {
}]);
```

3. Now we have the data to use with our table directive. Let's install the directive itself. In this example, we just use a CDN and only place the links on the `index.html` file:

```
<link rel="stylesheet" href="http://ui-grid.info/release/ui-grid-unstable.min.css">
<script src="http://ui-grid.info/release/ui-grid-unstable.min.js"></script>
```

4. Place the following links in the `index.html` file; CSS goes on top, inside the `head` tag, and JS goes after the `injector`'s-js link.

5. Add `ngGrid` to our `app.js` file:

```
angular.module('yeomananddirectives', [
    'ngResource',
    'ui.bootstrap',
    'ngCookies',
    'ngAnimate',
    'ngTouch',
    'ngSanitize',
    'ui.router',
    'mapping',
    'login',
    'ui.grid',
    'gridexample',
])
```

6. Let's add the directive to `griexample.html`:

```
<div class="container">
  <div ui-grid="gridOptions" style="width:100%;
  height:400px"></div>
</div>
```

7. Finally, let's add the controller's code:

```
$scope.myData = GridexampleService.query();

$scope.gridOptions = {
  data: 'myData',
  columnDefs: [
    {field: 'name', displayName: 'Name'},
    {field:'type', displayName:'Type'},
    { field: 'category', displayName: 'Category'},
    { field: 'brewer', displayName: 'Brewer'},
    { field: 'country', displayName: 'Country'}

  ]
};
```

> Note that we make a call to external API here. However, in development (using localhost) mode, we must enable CORS on the server, as we do not have access to the server configuration. So, we are using a static JSON file that simulates the original request to the API. You can check the code at `http://ontariobeerapi.ca:80/beers/`.

8. Run the `grunt dev` command and check your browser at the URL `http://127.0.0.1:8000/#!/gridexample`.

How it works...

The steps used here were very similar to the previous recipe, because almost all custom directives have the same step-by-step installation process.

However, in this example, we just added the external links to the CSS and JS directives files. On production applications, it is better to have total control over all dependencies, but we can use a CDN in this short example.

This grid component is very powerful and makes use of various directives. We can combine a variety of directives, such as `ui.grid`, `ui.grid.pagination`, and others, to build the whole grid.

Another important point is the `ui-grid="gridOptions"` object configuration. It's possible to make any setup combination here.

Implementing Custom Directives with Yeoman Generators

There's more...

We can set up a pagination very easily. Just add the following code to `gridexampleCtrl.js`:

```
$scope.gridOptions = {
  data: 'myData',
  paginationPageSizes: [25, 50, 75],
  paginationPageSize: 25,
  columnDefs: [
    {field: 'name', displayName: 'Name'},
    {field:'type', displayName:'Type'},
    { field: 'category', displayName: 'Category'},
    { field: 'brewer', displayName: 'Brewer'},
    { field: 'country', displayName: 'Country'}

  ]
};
```

Add the `ui.grid.pagination` module to the `app.js` file:

```
angular.module('yeomananddirectives', [
  'ngResource',
  'ui.bootstrap',
  'ngCookies',
  'ngAnimate',
  'ngTouch',
  'ngSanitize',
  'ui.router',
  'mapping',
  'login',
  'ui.grid',
  'ui.grid.pagination',
  'gridexample',
])
```

Finally, add the `ui.grid.pagination` attribute to the `gridexample.html` file:

```
<div ui-grid="gridOptions" ui-grid-pagination style="width:100%;
height:400px"></div>
```

The final result will be something like the following screenshot:

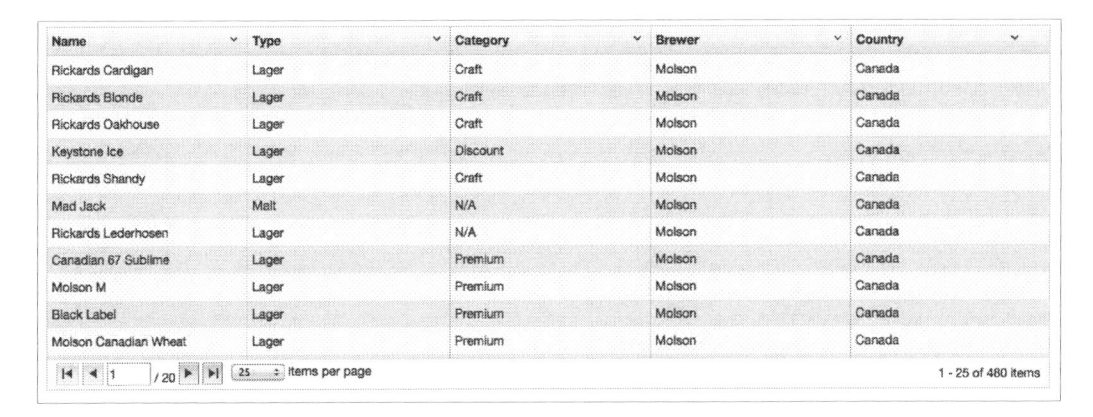

Name	Type	Category	Brewer	Country
Rickards Cardigan	Lager	Craft	Molson	Canada
Rickards Blonde	Lager	Craft	Molson	Canada
Rickards Oakhouse	Lager	Craft	Molson	Canada
Keystone Ice	Lager	Discount	Molson	Canada
Rickards Shandy	Lager	Craft	Molson	Canada
Mad Jack	Malt	N/A	Molson	Canada
Rickards Lederhosen	Lager	N/A	Molson	Canada
Canadian 67 Sublime	Lager	Premium	Molson	Canada
Molson M	Lager	Premium	Molson	Canada
Black Label	Lager	Premium	Molson	Canada
Molson Canadian Wheat	Lager	Premium	Molson	Canada

|◀ ◀ 1 /20 ▶ ▶| 25 ⇕ items per page   1 - 25 of 480 items

See also

▶ You can find out more about the ngGrid at `http://ui-grid.info/docs/#/api`

6
Using Directives to Develop Interface Components

In this chapter, we will cover:

- Creating an Off Canvas menu
- Applying custom CSS
- Building a shopping cart

Introduction

In this chapter, we will explain how to use AngularJS directives as interface components to build a micro e-commerce application combining different directives, an Off Canvas menu, customize directives style, and a shopping cart directive.

Creating an Off Canvas menu

Off Canvas menus are very common in web applications. In the age of mobiles, this is a flexible and useful component.

In the following recipe, we will see how to implement an Off Canvas directive.

> You can find more information about the Off Canvas menu at `https://github.com/dbtek/angular-aside`.

Using Directives to Develop Interface Components

Getting ready

Let's create a folder to hold the entire project and name it `interface-components`. Inside the folder, open your terminal window and type:

`yo angm`

With the previous command, the application will be generated with all the baseline code that we will need to start.

At the time of writing this chapter, the currently stable AngularJS version was v1.4.2. So, the generator-angm uses this version to create our application.

Now, let's implement the following recipes using the home module that is already installed.

How to do it...

1. The first step is to install a new directive. Open your terminal window and type the following command:

   `bower install angular-aside --save`

   Due to some version issues, we need to perform some options before we proceed. The following screenshot shows the options we need to choose:

   ```
   Unable to find a suitable version for angular, please choose one:
       1) angular#>=1 <1.3.0 which resolved to 1.2.28 and is required by angular-bootstrap#0.12.1
       2) angular#>=1.3.* which resolved to 1.4.2 and is required by interfacecomponents
       3) angular#>=1 which resolved to 1.4.2 and is required by angular-bootstrap#0.11.2
       4) angular#1.4.2 which resolved to 1.4.2 and is required by angular-resource#1.4.2
       5) angular#>= 1.0.8 which resolved to 1.4.2 and is required by angular-ui-router#0.2.15

   Prefix the choice with ! to persist it to bower.json

   ? Answer: 4

   Unable to find a suitable version for angular-bootstrap, please choose one:
       1) angular-bootstrap#~0.11.2 which resolved to 0.11.2 and is required by interfacecomponents
       2) angular-bootstrap#~0.12.0 which resolved to 0.12.1 and is required by angular-aside#1.1.3

   Prefix the choice with ! to persist it to bower.json

   ? Answer: 2
   bower install          angular#1.4.2
   bower install          angular-bootstrap#0.12.1
   bower install          angular-aside#1.1.3
   ```

   Another very important point is the word `--save` at the end of the command. If we forget to include this, the next step will fail.

2. On the terminal window, type the following command:

   `grunt injector`

   The following screenshot shows the result of the previous command:

   ```
   Running "injector:local_dependencies" (injector) task
   Missing option `template`, using `dest` as template instead
   Injecting css files (1 files)
   Injecting js files (19 files)

   Done, without errors.


   Execution Time (2015-07-11 15:31:42 UTC)
   loading tasks                  2.8s  ████████████████████████  62%
   injector:local_dependencies    1.7s  ███████████████  38%
   Total 4.6s
   ```

   In this step, skip the manual installation process covered in the previous chapter.

   > The `Gruntfile` has the task of taking care of it for us. As you can see in the previous screenshot, the generator already includes the CSS and JS files from the Angular-Aside directive to the `index.htm` file in the root of the application.

3. At this point, we have the directive ready to start, just check the `index.html` file to check if everything goes well.

   ```
   <link rel="stylesheet" href="/src/bower_components/angular-aside/dist/css/angular-aside.css">
   <script src="/src/bower_components/angular-aside/dist/js/angular-aside.js"></script>
   ```

4. Add the `ngAside` directive to the `app.js` file, like the following highlighted code:

   ```
   angular.module('interfacecomponents', [
       'ngResource',
       'ui.bootstrap',
       'ngCookies',
       'ngAnimate',
       'ngTouch',
       'ngSanitize',
       'ui.router',
       'ngAside'
   ])
   ```

Using Directives to Develop Interface Components

5. Let's replace the original code on `home.html` inside the `home` module with the following code:

```html
<div class="container">
  <div class="row">
    <div class="col-lg-12">
      <div ng-controller="HomeCtrl">
        <div class="text-center">
          <h1>{{ title }}</h1>
          <button class="btn btn-default" ng-click="openAside('left')">View Cart</button>
          <hr>
          <div class="row">
            <div class="col-xs-6 col-sm-3">
              <img src="https://placehold.it/262x150" alt="image" />
              <h4>My Item #1</h4>
              <p> $10.99</p>
              <div id="item1" name="My Item #1" price="10.99" quantity="1" quantity-max="5">Add to Cart</div>
            </div>
            <div class="col-xs-6 col-sm-3">
              <img src="https://placehold.it/262x150" alt="image" />
              <h4>My Item #2</h4>
              <p> $15.29</p>
              <div id="item2" name="My Item #2" price="15.29" quantity="1" quantity-max="5">Add to Cart</div>
            </div>
            <div class="col-xs-6 col-sm-3">
              <img src="https://placehold.it/262x150" alt="image" />
              <h4>My Item #3</h4>
              <p> $25.75</p>
              <div id="item3" name="My Item #3" price="25.75" quantity="3" quantity-max="10">Add to Cart</div>
            </div>
            <div class="col-xs-6 col-sm-3">
              <img src="https://placehold.it/262x150" alt="image" />
              <h4>My Item #4</h4>
              <p> $29.25</p>
```

```
                <div id="item4" name="My Item #4"
                price="29.25" quantity="1" quantity-
                max="10">Add to Cart</div>
              </div>
            </div>
          </div>
        </div>
      </div>
    </div>
  </div>
</div>
```

6. Replace the `homeCtrl.js` code with the following code:

   ```
   'use strict';

   /**
    * @ngdoc function
    * @name app.controller:HomeCtrl
    * @description
    * # HomeCtrl
    * Controller of the app
    */
   angular.module('interfacecomponents')
   .controller('HomeCtrl', ['$scope', '$aside', function
   ($scope, $aside) {
     $scope.title = "Interface Components";

     // Set default state of modal to close
     $scope.asideState = {
       open: false
     };

     // Activate the aside menu using the modal
     $scope.openAside = function(position, backdrop) {
       // Change the default close state
       $scope.asideState = {
         open: true,
         position: position
       };

       function postClose() {
         $scope.asideState.open = false;
       }
   ```

Using Directives to Develop Interface Components

```
            var modalInstance = $aside.open({
            templateUrl:
            'app/modules/shared/directives/offcanvas/aside.html',
            placement: position,
            size: 'sm',
            backdrop: backdrop,
            controller: 'AsideCtrl'
            }).result.then(postClose, postClose);
        }

}]);
```

Now we need to create two files, one to hold the `offcanvas` HTML template and another for the aside controller. Let's do it.

7. Create a folder called `directives` inside the `shared` folder of the `modules` folder. Create a folder called `offcanvas` inside the `directives` folder. Create a file called `aside.html` inside the `offcanvas` folder and place the following code:

```html
<div class="modal-header">
  <h3 class="modal-title">Shopping Cart</h3>
</div>
<div class="modal-body">
  <div class="alert alert-warning">
    <p>
      Your Cart is Empty
    </p>
  </div>
</div>
<div class="modal-footer">
  <button class="btn btn-primary">Checkout</button>
  <button class="btn btn-warning" ng-
  click="cancel()">Cancel</button>
</div>
```

8. Create a file called `asideCtrl.js` inside the `offcanvas` folder and place the following code in it:

```
'use strict';

/**
 * @ngdoc function
 * @name app.controller:AsideCtrl
 * @description
 * # AsideCtrl
 * Controller of the app
 */
```

Chapter 6

```
angular.module('interfacecomponents')
.controller('AsideCtrl', ['$scope', '$modalInstance',
function ($scope, $modalInstance) {

  // Close modal
  $scope.cancel = function () {
    $modalInstance.dismiss('cancel');
  };
}]);
```

9. After all these steps, we have the following layout:

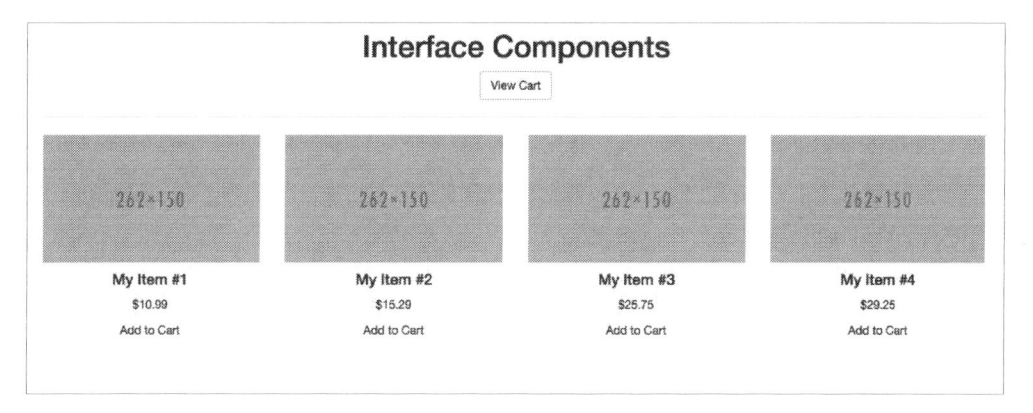

10. A pretty simple product layout. The `offcanvas` menu can be activated by pressing the **View Cart** button, as we can see on the following image:

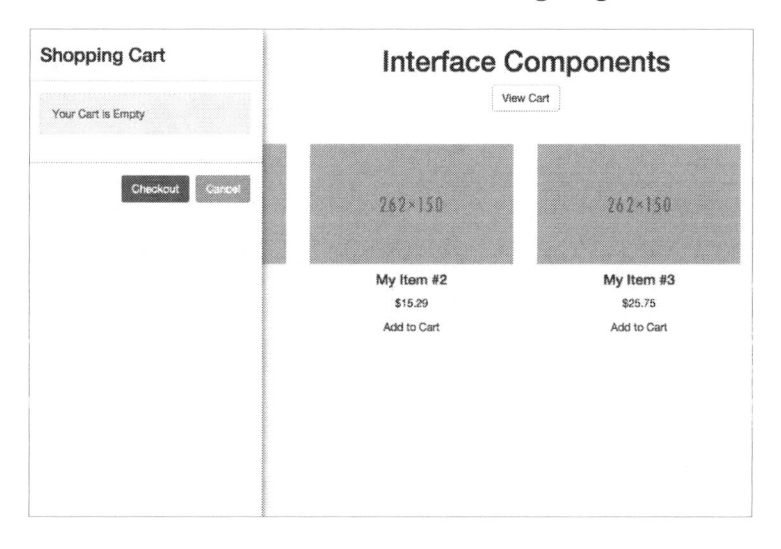

11. Just open your terminal window and type `grunt dev`, and your default browser will open.

Using Directives to Develop Interface Components

How it works...

We used a lot of code to create this layout page, which is similar to an e-commerce page. We used a combination of various directives, so let's understand what happened.

The installation process is very similar to the one we used in the previous chapters, except for the first step, where we need to choose some versions from AngularJS and other dependencies. This is because some versions are not 100 percent compatible with others.

This is common in large-scale applications, where we need to install different directives. As you know, AngularJS is growing fast and some packages don't stay up-to-date with the latest AngularJS version, so minor issues may occur.

The `ngAside` extends the `Angular ui boostrap` modal component and also depends on `ui.bootstrap.modal`. As we have already included `ui.bootstrap` in our project by default, this is not a problem.

The `ngAside` extends the modal with some new attribute `position` and uses all modal attributes available, as shown in the following block of code:

```
$scope.openAside = function(position, backdrop) {

  $scope.asideState = {
    open: true,
    position: position
  };
}
```

When modal is activated, we pass also the position inside the `ng-click` modal function:

```
ng-click="openAside('left')"
```

In the previous code, we can pass an optional backdrop as a second parameter:

```
ng-click="openAside('left', true)"
```

This way, we have a dark background under the aside menu, very similar to modal components, where we have a dark transparent background.

The home controller receives the `$aside` instance as a dependency:

```
.controller('HomeCtrl', ['$scope', '$aside', function ($scope, $aside) {}
```

The instantiate method is the same for modal, except we use `$aside.open` instead of `$modal.open`:

```
var modalInstance = $aside.open({
})
```

In this example, we have set up an external template and controller for better customized options:

```
var modalInstance = $aside.open({
  templateUrl:
  'app/modules/shared/directives/offcanvas/aside.html',
  placement: position,
  size: 'sm',
  backdrop: backdrop,
  controller: 'AsideCtrl'
})
```

See also

▸ You can see more about the ui.bootstrap modal at the official webpage http://angular-ui.github.io/bootstrap/#/modal

Applying custom CSS

In this recipe, we will see how we can apply some CSS style to directives. In this special case, we will override the default Bootstrap CSS style, as we are building an e-commerce layout. Let's see how to customize the Off Canvas menu directive.

Getting ready

We will use the same code base from the previous chapter. So, we just add some CSS styles to the application.

How to do it...

1. Inside the `assets/css` folder, create a file called `style.css`. Add the `style.css` code to the `index.html` file after the injector tag:

   ```
   <!-- injector:css -->
   <link rel="stylesheet" href="/src/bower_components/bootstrap/dist/css/bootstrap.css">
   <link rel="stylesheet" href="/src/bower_components/angular-aside/dist/css/angular-aside.css">
   <!-- endinjector -->
   <link rel="stylesheet" href="/app/assets/css/style.css">
   ```

2. Place the following code into the `style.css` file:

   ```
   .modal-header {
     min-height: 16.42857143px;
     padding: 15px;
   ```

```css
  border-bottom: 1px solid #B8B6B6;
  background-color: #EAEAEA;
  text-align: center;
}

.modal-body {
  position: relative;
  padding: 15px;
  background-color: #F4F4F4;
  min-height: 400px;
}

.modal-footer {
  padding: 15px;
  text-align: right;
  border-top: 1px solid #B8B6B6;
  background-color: #EAEAEA;

  position: absolute;
  bottom: 0px;
  width: 100%;
  text-align: center;
}
```

Now, the Off Canvas menu looks like this:

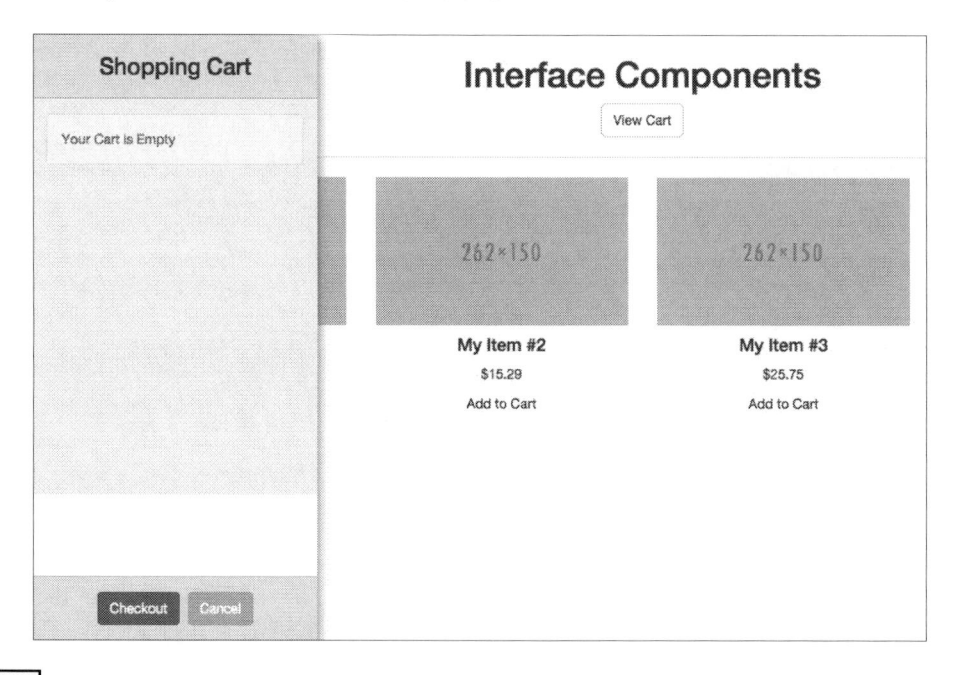

How it works...

The process used to style the aside menu known as Off Canvas is very simple.

We insert the link to the new stylesheet created in step 1, right after the injector tag. This is shown in the following example:

```
<!-- injector:css →
<!-- endinjector -->
```

This is due to the fact that every time we run a task from `Grunt.js`, everything between the injector tag is replaced by the dependencies declared in our `bower.json` file.

We just used three modal classes to apply the style. Also, we used the Bootstrap default class for `alert-warning`.

There's more...

We can use custom CSS directly on Bootstrap internals using LESS files. To do that, follow the steps given earlier.

You can find the Bootstrap modal files at the following path:

```
Project Folder
|-src/
|--bower_components/
|---bootstrap/
|----less/
|-----modal.less
```

Here we use the variables of LESS to apply a new style to our modal:

```
//== Modals
//
//##

//** Padding applied to the modal body
@modal-inner-padding:         15px;

//** Padding applied to the modal title
@modal-title-padding:         15px;
//** Modal title line-height
@modal-title-line-height:     @line-height-base;

//** Background color of modal content area
```

Using Directives to Develop Interface Components

```
@modal-content-bg:                              #fff;
//** Modal content border color
@modal-content-border-color:                    rgba(0,0,0,.2);
//** Modal content border color **for IE8**
@modal-content-fallback-border-color:           #999;

//** Modal backdrop background color
@modal-backdrop-bg:             #000;
//** Modal backdrop opacity
@modal-backdrop-opacity:        .5;
//** Modal header border color
@modal-header-border-color:     #e5e5e5;
//** Modal footer border color
@modal-footer-border-color:     @modal-header-border-color;

@modal-lg:                      900px;
@modal-md:                      600px;
@modal-sm:                      300px;
```

The previous variables can be found at the root of the Bootstrap folder in a file called `variables.less`.

See also

- You can read more about LESS at the following URL http://lesscss.org/

Building a shopping cart

In the previous chapter, we used an example of e-commerce to illustrate the operation of the Off Canvas menu, implementing a shopping cart. In this recipe, we will use a custom directive to add functionality to the **Add to Cart** and **View Cart** buttons.

Getting ready

Let's use the same example from the previous chapter, where we finalized with CSS customization.

How to do it...

1. First off, we need to install the shopping cart directive. As in the previous recipe, we will install it with Bower. Open your terminal window at the project root and type the following command:

   `bower install ngcart --save`

   > If you do not use the Bower dependencies manager, you can add the directive to the project manually, as previously taught in earlier chapters.

2. Now, open the `app` folder and edit the `app.js` file. Add the following highlighted code after the `ngAside` dependency:

   ```
   angular.module('interfacecomponents', [
     'ngResource',
     'ui.bootstrap',
     'ngCookies',
     'ngAnimate',
     'ngTouch',
     'ngSanitize',
     'ui.router',
     'ngAside',
     'ngCart'
   ])
   ```

3. Let's create a `ngCart` controller. Go to `modules/shared/directives/` and create a folder called `ngcart`. Inside this folder, create a file called `ngcartCtrl.js` and add the following code:

   ```
   'use strict';

   /**
    * @ngdoc function
    * @name app.controller:ShopCartCtrl
    * @description
    * # ShopCartCtrl
    * Controller of the app
    */
   angular.module('interfacecomponents')
   .controller('ShopCartCtrl', ['$scope', 'ngCart', '$http',
   function ($scope, ngCart, $http) {
   ```

Using Directives to Develop Interface Components

```
     ngCart.setTaxRate(7.5);
      ngCart.setShipping(2.99);

}]);
```

4. With the third step, we finished the installation process and initialization of `ngCart`. Let's move on to the next steps. Edit the `home.html` file, remove the column layout with products, and place a new div with `ShopCartCtrl`. This is shown in the following code:

```html
<div ng-controller="ShopCartCtrl">
  <div class="row text-center">
    <div class="col-xs-6 col-sm-3">
      <img src="https://placehold.it/262x150" alt="image"
      />
      <h4>My Item #1</h4>
      <p> $10.99</p>
      <ngcart-addtocart id="item1" name="My Item #1"
      price="10.99" quantity="1" quantity-max="5">Add to
      Cart</ngcart-addtocart>
    </div>
    <div class="col-xs-6 col-sm-3">
      <img src="https://placehold.it/262x150" alt="image"
      />
      <h4>My Item #2</h4>
      <p> $15.29</p>
      <ngcart-addtocart id="item2" name="My Item #2"
      price="15.29" quantity="1" quantity-max="5">Add to
      Cart</ngcart-addtocart>
    </div>
      <div class="col-xs-6 col-sm-3">
      <img src="https://placehold.it/262x150" alt="image"
      />
      <h4>My Item #3</h4>
      <p> $25.75</p>
      <ngcart-addtocart id="item3" name="My Item #3"
      price="25.75" quantity="3" quantity-max="10">Add to
      Cart</ngcart-addtocart>
    </div>
    <div class="col-xs-6 col-sm-3">
      <img src="https://placehold.it/262x150" alt="image"
      />
      <h4>My Item #4</h4>
      <p> $29.25</p>
      <ngcart-addtocart id="item4" name="My Item #4"
      price="29.25" quantity="1" quantity-max="10">Add to
      Cart</ngcart-addtocart>
```

```
      </div>
    </div>
</div>
```

5. Note that we replace the div from the previous example with the `ngcart-addtocart` directive on the highlighted code. Add the `addtocart` template at the end of `home.html` file:

```
<script type="text/ng-template"
id="template/ngCart/addtocart.html">
<div ng-hide="attrs.id">
  <a class="btn btn-lg btn-primary" ng-disabled="true" ng-
  transclude></a>
</div>
<div ng-show="attrs.id">
  <div>
    <span ng-show="quantityMax">
      <select name="quantity" id="quantity" ng-model="q"
      ng-options=" v for v in qtyOpt"></select>
    </span>
      <a class="btn btn-sm btn-primary" ng-
      click="ngCart.addItem(id, name, price, q, data)" ng-
      transclude></a>
  </div>
  <span ng-show="inCart()">
  <br>
  <p class="alert alert-info">This item is in your cart. <a
  ng-click="ngCart.removeItemById(id)" style="cursor:
  pointer;">Remove</a></p>
  </span>
</div>
</script>
```

6. Go back to your terminal window and type the following command:

   grunt dev

   At this point, we will have an e-commerce layout with the `ngcart` directive:

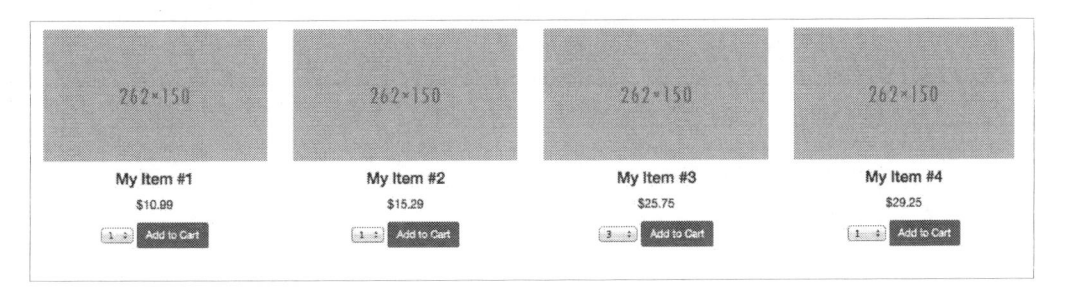

Using Directives to Develop Interface Components

7. Now we need to add the cart summary using the `ngcart-summary` directive. Add the following line after the `shopcartctrl div` controller:

    ```
    <div ng-controller="ShopCartCtrl">
    <div class="well text-center"><ngcart-summary></ngcart-summary></div>
    ...
    ```

8. Add the cart summary template at the end of `home.html` file, after the `add to cart` template:

    ```
    <script type="text/ng-template" id="template/ngCart/summary.html">
      <span class="">{{ ngCart.getTotalItems() }}
        <ng-pluralize count="ngCart.getTotalItems()" when="{1:
        'item', 'other':'items'}"></ng-pluralize>
        <br />{{ ngCart.totalCost() | currency }}
      </span>
    </script>
    ```

    The previous operation will result in the following screenshot:

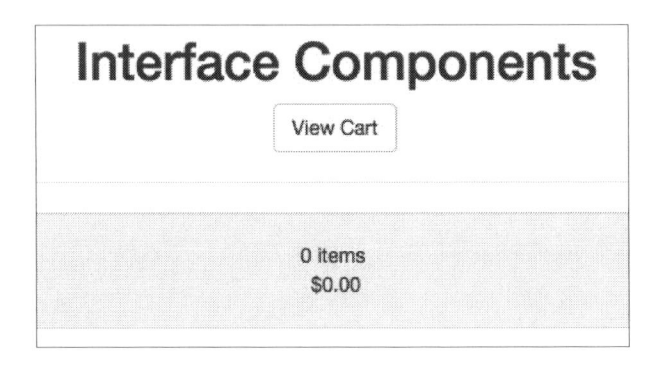

    Interface Components

    View Cart

    0 items
    $0.00

9. Let's edit `aside.html` to include the cart itself. Inside the `modal-body` div, replace `div alert` with the following code:

    ```
    <div class="modal-body">
      <ngcart-cart></ngcart-cart>
    </div>
    ```

10. Add the cart template to the end of the `aside.html` file using the following code:

    ```
    <script type="text/ng-template" id="template/ngCart/cart.html">
    <div class="alert alert-warning" role="alert" ng-show="ngCart.getTotalItems() === 0">
      Your cart is empty
    </div>
    <div class="table-responsive col-lg-12" ng-show="ngCart.getTotalItems() > 0">
    ```

```html
<table class="table table-striped ngCart cart">
  <thead>
    <tr>
      <th></th>
      <th></th>
      <th>Quantity</th>
      <th>Amount</th>
      <th>Total</th>
    </tr>
  </thead>
  <tfoot>
    <tr ng-show="ngCart.getTax()">
      <td></td>
      <td></td>
      <td></td>
      <td>Tax ({{ ngCart.getTaxRate() }}%):</td>
      <td>{{ ngCart.getTax() | currency }}</td>
    </tr>
    <tr ng-show="ngCart.getShipping()">
      <td></td>
      <td></td>
      <td></td>
      <td>Shipping:</td>
      <td>{{ ngCart.getShipping() | currency }}</td>
    </tr>
    <tr>
      <td></td>
      <td></td>
      <td></td>
      <td>Total:</td>
      <td>{{ ngCart.totalCost() | currency }}</td>
    </tr>
  </tfoot>
  <tbody>
    <tr ng-repeat="item in ngCart.getCart().items track
    by $index">
      <td><span ng-
      click="ngCart.removeItemById(item.getId())"
      class="glyphicon glyphicon-remove"></span></td>

      <td>{{ item.getName() }}</td>
      <td><span class="glyphicon glyphicon-minus" ng-
      class="{'disabled':item.getQuantity()==1}"
      ng-click="item.setQuantity(-1,
      true)"></span>  
```

Using Directives to Develop Interface Components

```
        {{ item.getQuantity() | number }}  
        <span class="glyphicon glyphicon-plus" ng-
        click="item.setQuantity(1, true)"></span></td>
        <td>{{ item.getPrice() | currency}}</td>
        <td>{{ item.getTotal() | currency }}</td>
      </tr>
    </tbody>
  </table>
</div>
</script>
```

11. The last action is to add the checkout functionality. Let's add the template code to the end of `aside.html`, right after the cart template:

    ```
    <script type="text/ng-template"
    id="template/ngCart/checkout.html">
    <span ng-if="service=='http' || service == 'log'">
      <button class="btn btn-primary" ng-click="checkout()" ng-
      disabled="!ngCart.getTotalItems()" ng-
      transclude>Checkout</button>
    </span>
    </script>
    ```

12. Replace the `checkout` bottom inside the `modal-footer` div on `aside.html` with the following code:

    ```
    <div class="modal-footer">
      <ngcart-checkout service="log">Checkout</ngcart-checkout>
      <button class="btn btn-warning" ng-
      click="cancel()">Cancel</button>
    </div>
    ```

Now, let's check the final result. Open your terminal window and type the following command:

grunt dev

How it works...

We can see how to convert a static layout using custom directives. You can easily see this with the substitution of the code that creates the buttons to add the item to the shopping cart:

```
<div id="item1" name="My Item #1" price="10.99" quantity="1"
quantity-max="5">Add to Cart</div>
<ngcart-addtocart id="item1" name="My Item #1" price="10.99"
quantity="1" quantity-max="5">Add to Cart</ngcart-addtocart>
```

> In this example, we kept fixed products in the HTML code, but in a real application they would be in a database and would use some Ajax function to retrieve them.

As we did in the previous recipes, we are using custom templates here:

```
<script type="text/ng-template"
id="template/ngCart/addtocart.html"></script>
<script type="text/ng-template"
id="template/ngCart/summary.html"></script>
<script type="text/ng-template"
id="template/ngCart/cart.html"></script>
<script type="text/ng-template"
id="template/ngCart/checkout.html"></script>
```

This flexibility is provided by the `ngCart` directives. When we click on the **Add to Cart** button, the directive shows a simple message. This is shown in the following screenshot:

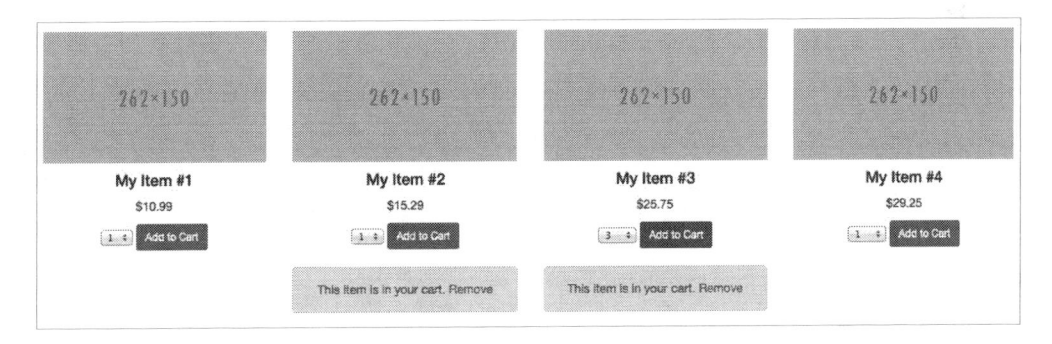

It's possible to add and remove a product using the directive's add to cart function:

```
<a class="btn btn-sm btn-primary"
  ng-click="ngCart.addItem(id, name, price, q, data)"
  ng-transclude></a>
```

The products are stored using the local storage of your browser, which is the built in `store service` feature from directive:

```
.service('store', ['$window', function ($window) {
return {

  get: function (key) {
    if ($window.localStorage [key]) {
      var cart = angular.fromJson($window.localStorage [key]);
```

```
      return JSON.parse(cart);
    }
    return false;
  },

  set: function (key, val) {

    if (val === undefined) {
      $window.localStorage .removeItem(key);
    } else {
      $window.localStorage [key] = angular.toJson(val);
    }
    return $window.localStorage [key];
  }
}
}])
```

The following screenshot shows the result of clicking on the **View Cart** button:

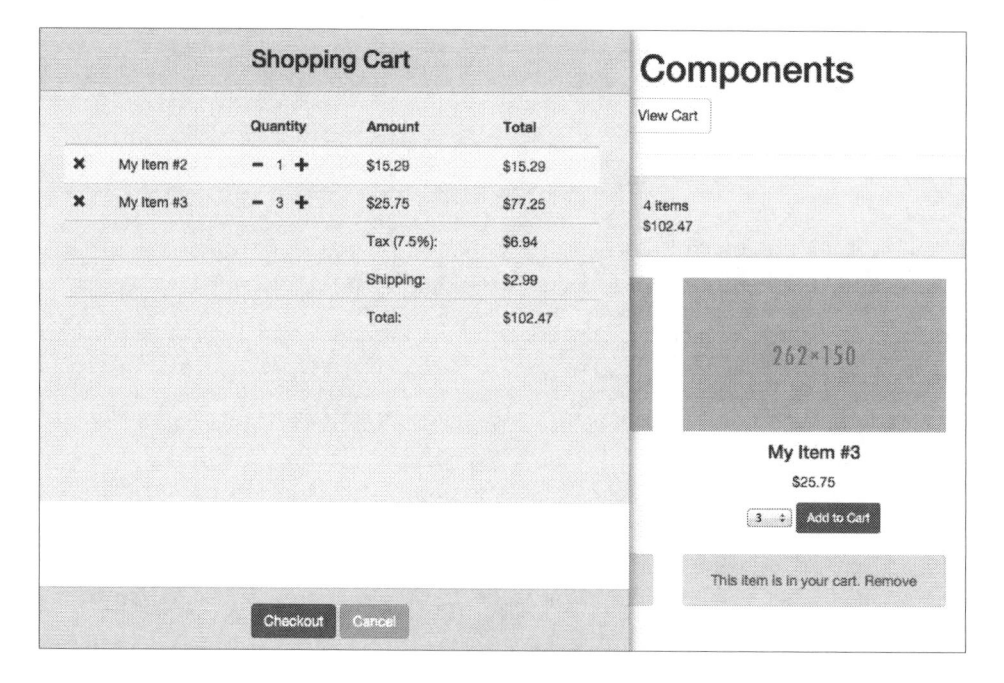

Chapter 6

The **Checkout** button can perform three different tasks, including integration with PayPal. For this recipe, we just use `$log`.

When we click on the **Checkout** button, the result for shopping cart can be found at the console panel of your browser, as we can see in the following screenshot:

```
▼Object {shipping: 2.99, tax: 6.94, taxRate: 7.5, subTotal: 92.54, totalCost: 102.47…}
  ▼items: Array[2]
    ▼0: Object
        data: undefined
        id: "item2"
        name: "My Item #2"
        price: 15.29
        quantity: 1
        total: 15.29
      ▶__proto__: Object
    ▼1: Object
        data: undefined
        id: "item3"
        name: "My Item #3"
        price: 25.75
        quantity: 3
        total: 77.25
      ▶__proto__: Object
      length: 2
    ▶__proto__: Array[0]
    shipping: 2.99
    subTotal: 92.54
    tax: 6.94
    taxRate: 7.5
    totalCost: 102.47
  ▶__proto__: Object
```

> Note that the attribute data is empty just because we used a simple example to illustrate the directive functionality in an e-commerce application. On real applications, this contains an object with attributes from the item.

There's more...

We can extend the directive and add more properties to our product just by editing the `ngCart` directive and by adding as many properties as we need:

```
.directive('ngcartAddtocart', ['ngCart', function(ngCart){
    return {
        restrict : 'E',
        controller : 'CartController',
        scope: {
            id:'@',
            name:'@',
            quantity:'@',
```

115

Using Directives to Develop Interface Components

```
        quantityMax:'@',
        price:'@',
        data:'='
    },
...
```

Also, it's possible to use a service to load the products list from a JSON file like this:

```
[
    {
      "id": 01,
      "name": "Item 1",
      "price": 1900,
      "image": :"https://placehold.it/262x150"
    },
    {
      "id": 02,
      "name": "Item 2",
      "price": 1000,
      "image": :"https://placehold.it/262x150"
    },
    {
      "id": 03,
      "name": "Item 3",
      "price": 900,
      "image": :"https://placehold.it/262x150"
    }
]
```

Then, replace the cart items with the following code:

```html
<div class="col-xs-6 col-sm-3" ng-repeat=" item in products">
  <img src="{{item.image}}" alt="image" />
  <h4>{{item.name}}</h4>
  <p> ${{item.price}}</p>
  <ngcart-addtocart id="{{item.id}}" name="{{item.name}}"
  price="{{item.price}}" quantity="1" quantity-max="5">Add to
  Cart</ngcart-addtocart>
</div>
```

7
Building Directives with Dynamic Templates

In this chapter, we will cover:

- Using dynamic templates on directives
- The compile function
- Organizing dynamic directives on shared folders
- Mixing different content on templates

Introduction

Dealing with dynamic templates on directives is not a common task with AngularJS, because we can change the style of a view directly with CSS, but often this is a technique that can help us to implement a different direction, and leave us with different and flexible templates. It is always very helpful to have different options at hand.

In this chapter, we will see an easy way to implement this technique with AngularJS in two different stages, the first using an inline template inside the directive using the $compile function, and another using external templates.

This chapter is somewhat conceptual and may seem to escape the cookbook format, but here we present some features and techniques that are related to all the recipes in this chapter.

The total content is a powerful way to deal with directives using dynamic templates.

Building Directives with Dynamic Templates

Using dynamic templates on directives

In this first example we will create a directive using inline templates rendered by the JavaScript inside of the directive. Also, in the example we will simulate the `$http.get()` method to get the closest example of a real situation.

In addition, we will see an important tip for loading videos from external sources using our application on a local server.

Getting ready

We are still using the Yeoman generator-angm (version 0.2.6) to build the base line application. You can get the code in the examples folder at PacktPub, or open your terminal window and type:

```
yo angm
```

Name it `dynamic-templates` and press *Enter*, *Enter*, and *Enter*..

> The generator-angm (version 0.2.6) uses the new stable version from AngularJS, 1.4.5. For this chapter, it is very important to use the same version because on the next release, the generator will have some major changes and will use a different approach to build AngularJS modular applications.

How to do it...

1. Before we start to code, let's add the baseline folders and files. In the `modules/shared/` folder, create a folder called `directives`, and inside that folder create a folder called `dynamic-template`; the full path will be `modules/shared/directives/dynamic-template`.

2. For the first example, let's create two files. Inside `modules/shared/directives/dynamic-template`, create a file and name it `dynamic-template-directive.js`. Note that you can use your own name, but to follow the example, we recommend keeping with the book names. Create a new file in the same folder and name it `content.json`.

3. Now, let's add the code to both files. Place the following code in `dynamic-template-directive.js`:

   ```
   'use strict';
   
   /**
    * @ngdoc function
   ```

```
 * @name app.directive:DynamicTemplateDirective
 * @description
 * # dynamicTemplateDirective
 * Directive of the app
 */
angular.module('dynamic-templates')
.directive('contentItem', function ($compile) {

  var imageTpl = '<div class="media"><div class="media-
  left"><a href="{{content.src}}"><img class="media-object
  img-thumbnail" ng-src="{{content.src}}"
  alt="content.title"></a></div><div class="media-body"><h2
  class="media-heading">{{content.title}}</h2>
  <p>{{content.description}}</p></div></div>';
  var videoTpl = '<div class="entry-
  video"><h2>{{content.title}}</h2><div class="entry-
  vid"><iframe ng-src="{{content.src}}" width="100%"
  height="300" frameborder="0" webkitAllowFullScreen
  mozallowfullscreen allowFullScreen></iframe></div><div
  class="entry-text"><div class="text-
  justify">{{content.description}}</div></div></div>';
  var textTpl = '<div class="panel panel-default"><div
  class="panel-body"><h1>{{content.title}}</h1><p
  class="lead">{{content.src}}</p></div></div>';

  var getTemplate = function(type) {
    var template = '';

    switch(type) {
      case 'image':
      template = imageTpl;
      break;
      case 'video':
      template = videoTpl;
      break;
      case 'text':
      template = textTpl;
      break;
    }

    return template;
  }

  var linkF = function(scope, element, attrs) {
    element.html(getTemplate(scope.content.type)).show();
```

Building Directives with Dynamic Templates

```
      $compile(element.contents())(scope);
    }

    return {
      restrict: "E",
      link: linkF,
      scope: {
        content:'='
      }
    };
});
```

4. Place the following code on `content.json`:

   ```
   [
       {"type" : "image", "title" : "Black Label Society", "src" : "https://upload.wikimedia.org/wikipedia/en/b/bd/Sonic_Brew_Original_Cover.jpg", "description": "Lorem ipsum dolor sit amet, consectetur adipiscing elit, sed do eiusmod tempor incididunt ut labore et dolore magna aliqua. Ut enim ad minim veniam, quis nostrud exercitation ullamco laboris nisi ut aliquip ex ea commodo consequat. Duis aute irure dolor in reprehenderit in voluptate velit esse cillum dolore eu fugiat nulla pariatur."},
       {"type" : "video", "title" : "The One Motorcycle Video", "src" : "http://player.vimeo.com/video/60049452"},
       {"type" : "text", "title" : "Hunter S. Thompson, Hell's Angels: A Strange and Terrible Saga", "src" : "The Edge... There is no honest way to explain it because the only people who really know where it is are the ones who have gone over."},
       {"type" : "image", "title" : "Chrome Division", "src" : "https://upload.wikimedia.org/wikipedia/en/e/e8/Booze%2C_Broads_%26_Beelzebub_-_Chrome_Division.jpg", "description":"Lorem ipsum dolor sit amet, consectetur adipiscing elit, sed do eiusmod tempor incididunt ut labore et dolore magna aliqua. Ut enim ad minim veniam, quis nostrud exercitation ullamco laboris nisi ut aliquip ex ea commodo consequat. Duis aute irure dolor in reprehenderit in voluptate velit esse cillum dolore eu fugiat nulla pariatur."}
   ]
   ```

5. The first stage of the first example is almost done, so let's add some code on other files. Open the `home.html` file inside the `home` module at `app/modules/home/` and replace the original code with the following lines:

   ```
   <div class="container">
     <div class="splash text-center">
       <h1>{{ title }}</h1>
   ```

Chapter 7

```html
      <p>This is a template for a simple home screen website.
      Use it as a starting point to create something more
      unique.</p>
      <code>app/modules/home/home.html</code>
      <hr>
    </div>
    <br>
    <div class="row">
      <content-item ng-repeat="item in content"
      content="item"></content-item>
    </div>
  </div>
```

We just keep the original markup and add more content, but to avoid mistakes, replace the entire code.

> Note that the home module is part of the building process when we build any application with generator-angm.

6. The next step is to create the controller and grab the content from the content.json file. Let's replace the original content in homeCtrl.js with the following code:

```javascript
'use strict';

/**
 * @ngdoc function
 * @name app.controller:HomeCtrl
 * @description
 * # HomeCtrl
 * Controller of the app
 */
angular.module('dynamic-templates')
.controller('HomeCtrl', ['$scope', '$http', function
($scope, $http) {
  $scope.title = "Hello, Angm-Generator!";

  $scope.url = 'app/modules/shared/directives/dynamic-
  template/content.json';

  $scope.content = [];

  $scope.getContentFromFile = function() {
    $http.get($scope.url).then(function(result){
```

```
      $scope.content = result.data;
    });
  }
  $scope.getContentFromFile();
}]);
```

The last and most important step is to use the `$sceDelegateProvider` to ensure that the URLs required by the template of the directive are safe.

7. You can read more about the `$sceDelegate` in the official AngularJS documentation at https://docs.angularjs.org/api/ng/provider/$sceDelegateProvider. Open the app.js file in the root folder and add the following highlighted code:

```
'use strict';

/**
 * @ngdoc index
 * @name app
 * @description
 * # app
 *
 * Main module of the application.
 */
angular.module('dynamic-templates', [
  'ngResource',
  'ui.bootstrap',
  'ngCookies',
  'ngAnimate',
  'ngTouch',
  'ngSanitize',
  'ui.router'
])

  .config(['$stateProvider', '$urlRouterProvider',
'$locationProvider', '$httpProvider', '$sceDelegateProvider',
function ($stateProvider, $urlRouterProvider, $locationProvider,
$httpProvider, $sceDelegateProvider) {

    // Allow working on localhost or to avoid the video don't
    work properly
    $sceDelegateProvider.resourceUrlWhitelist(['self', '**']);

    $locationProvider.hashPrefix('!');

    // This is required for Browser Sync to work properly
```

```
        $httpProvider.defaults.headers.common['X-Requested-With']
        = 'XMLHttpRequest';

        $urlRouterProvider
           .otherwise('/');
    }])
    .run(['$rootScope', function ($rootScope) {

      'use strict';

      console.log('AngularJS run() function...');

    }]);
```

8. The last step is to start the application and see the final result in the browser. Open your terminal window at the root application folder and type the following command:

   grunt dev

Right after the welcome message on the home screen we can see the content from `content.json` rendered with different templates, one for each type of content.

The following image illustrates the result:

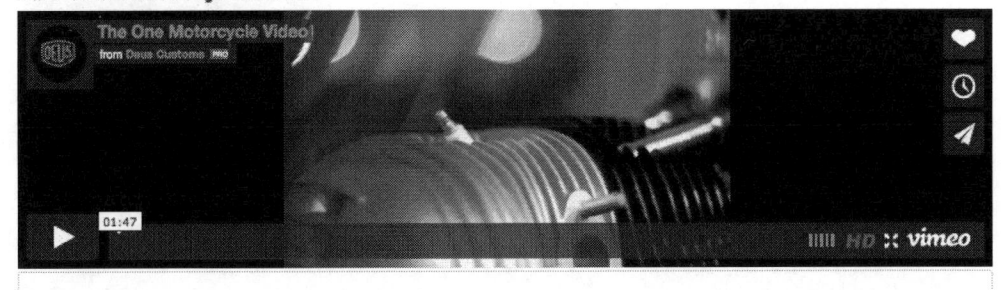

Building Directives with Dynamic Templates

How it works...

The directive is pretty simple but powerful. In the first step, we created the templates, but note that we don't use the built-in `templateCache` from AngularJS, we just place the templates inside the variables:

```
var imageTpl = '…'
var videoTpl = '…'
var textTpl = '…'
```

The reason is simple. We will call these variables inside the function to choose the right template based on the type:

```
var getTemplate = function(type) {
  var template = '';

  switch(type) {
    case 'image':
    template = imageTpl;
    break;
    case 'video':
    template = videoTpl;
    break;
    case 'text':
    template = textTpl;
    break;
  }

  return template;
}
```

For each type, we return a different template.

Also, we create a `linker` function and pass the name of the `link function` to the directive:

```
var linkF = function(scope, element, attrs) {…}
return {
  restrict: "E",
  link: linkF,
  scope: {
    content:'='
  }
};
```

The `scope:{ content:'='}` will be replaced on the directive markup declaration:

```
<content-item ng-repeat="item in content"
content="item"></content-item>
```

Also, on directive declaration, we are using the built-in `ng-repeat` directive to make a loop over our data, in this case `$scope.content` in `homeCtrl.js`:

```
$scope.content = [];

$scope.getContentFromFile = function() {
  $http.get($scope.url).then(function(result){
    $scope.content = result.data;
  });
}

$scope.getContentFromFile();
```

In this recipe, we are using a `$http.get()` to simulate a RESTful/Ajax request. In our case, we are reading data from a local file, but in a real application you would read data from an endpoint on a server. The data we get back will be formatted as JSON and have the following structure:

```
{
  "type" : "image",
  "title" : "Black Label Society",
  "src" :"image.jpg",
  "description": "..."
},
```

There's more...

A real service can have as many properties as you want and we can use the `$resource` feature to return our data, as we can see in the later recipe, *Mixing different content on templates*.

The compile function

In the previous recipes in previous chapters we mentioned the `$compile` function using the compile complete recommended syntax, as follows:

```
compile: function compile(tElement, tAttrs, transclude) {
  return {
    pre: function preLink(scope, iElement, iAttrs, controller) {
    ... },
    post: function postLink(scope, iElement, iAttrs, controller) {
    ... }
  }
}
```

In this recipe, we will show the alternative method of calling and using the `$compile` function.

Building Directives with Dynamic Templates

Getting ready

The baseline code for this recipe is the same as in the previous chapter.

How to do it...

As we are using the same code base, and we already wrote the code in the previous recipe, open the `dynamic-template-directive.js` and take a look at the `linkF` function:

```
var linkF = function(scope, element, attrs) {
  element.html(getTemplate(scope.content.type)).show();
  $compile(element.contents())(scope);
}
```

How it works...

Note that inside the `linkF`, we used the `.html()` and `.show()` methods from jQuery Lite (built in to AngularJS) to show and compile an element using the `$compile` function.

In this example, we don't use the `replace()` and `transclude()` AngularJS method, which will be deprecated on the next major (2.0) release from AngularJS.

See also

- You can find more about AngularJS's upcoming new version 2.0 at the official website: https://angular.io/docs/js/latest/api/

Organizing dynamic directives on shared folders

As the title suggests, dynamic directives in shared folders can become a nuisance in large-scale applications, as they are hard to maintain and hard to scale.

Also, keeping dynamic templates in JS files is not a very flexible way to structure and maintain the application.

This recipe is connected directly to what comes next, since we use the structure as an example to show the flexibility that can be achieved by prioritizing performance and easy maintenance.

Getting ready

The baseline code for this recipe is the same as in the previous chapter.

How to do it...

As we have mentioned in previous chapters, an easy way to group files in an application is to keep them united by features. Thus, nothing could be easier than keeping all files related to a directive in the same place.

But what do you do when you need to use the same file or template, since we are talking about dynamic templates?

A simple and efficient way to do this is to use the directive of `ng-include` in a custom directive to determine random templates for each type of content that your application may have.

Observe the following screenshot. We keep all template files externally directive and name each according to the content that will render on the screen, shown as follows:

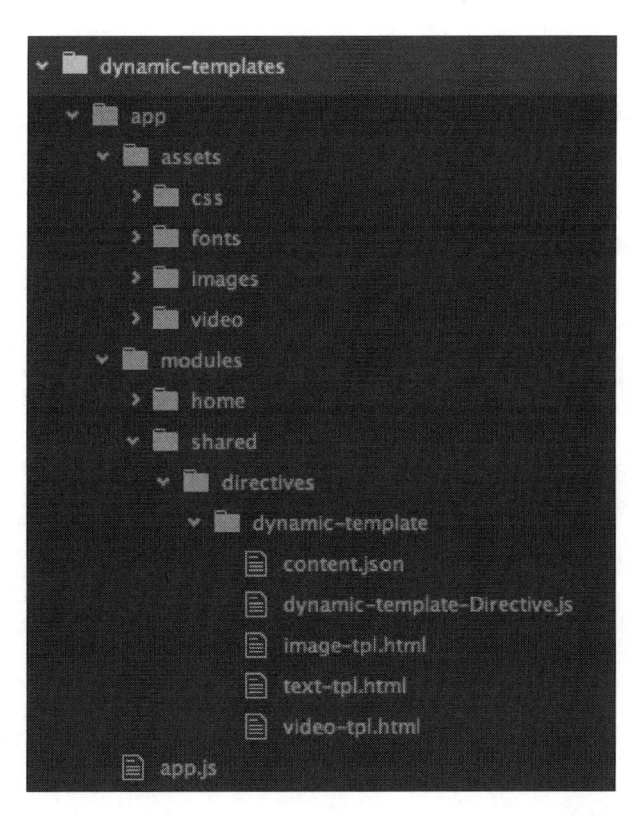

```
▼ ■ dynamic-templates
   ▼ ■ app
      ▼ ■ assets
         ▶ ■ css
         ▶ ■ fonts
         ▶ ■ images
         ▶ ■ video
      ▼ ■ modules
         ▶ ■ home
         ▼ ■ shared
            ▼ ■ directives
               ▼ ■ dynamic-template
                  ≡ content.json
                  ≡ dynamic-template-Directive.js
                  ≡ image-tpl.html
                  ≡ text-tpl.html
                  ≡ video-tpl.html
   ≡ app.js
```

Building Directives with Dynamic Templates

How it works...

The content from templates must have the same general notation on each controller function:

```
<div>
  <iframe width="300" height="300" ng-src="{{item.src}}"
  frameborder="0" allowfullscreen></iframe>
  <h2>{{item.name}}</h2>
</div>
```

This means that you must use generic names such as item.name, item.title, and item.description, as these names are very common for these types of applications and services. This way, we can use any controller.

Mixing different content on templates

Continuing with the previous example of organizing code, we can continue and create as many templates as necessary for the dynamic directives.

We will see in this example the use of ng-include, a built-in AngularJS directive using external templates, created in specific files, thus facilitating easy maintenance and scalability.

Also, we will see a different way to load the content using the $resource service in our controller function.

Getting ready

The baseline code for this recipe is the same as in the previous chapter. We just need to create additional files.

For the purpose of this book, we will place the new directive in the same file as the previous one. In a real application, we strongly recommend the use of one file per directive.

How to do it...

1. Open the dynamic-template-directive.js and add the following code at the end of the contentItem directive:

   ```
   angular.module('dynamic-templates')
   .directive('contentItem', function ($compile) {
      ....
   }).directive("postItem", function() {
     return {
       template: '<ng-include src="getTemplateUrl()"/>',
   ```

```
          //templateUrl: unfortunately has no access to
          $scope.user.type
          scope: {
            item: '=data'
          },
          restrict: 'E',
          controller: function($scope) {
            //function used on the ng-include to resolve the
            template
            $scope.getTemplateUrl = function() {
              //basic handling. It could be delegated to
              different Services
              if ($scope.item.type == "image")
                return "app/modules/shared/directives/dynamic-
                template/image-tpl.html";
              if ($scope.item.type == "video")
                return "app/modules/shared/directives/dynamic-
                template/video-tpl.html";
              if ($scope.item.type == "text")
                return "app/modules/shared/directives/dynamic-
                template/text-tpl.html";
            }
          }
        };
    });
```

2. Let's create the `image-tpl.html` file in the same folder of `dynamic-template-directive.js` and place the following code:

```
<div class="row">
  <div class="thum">
    <div class="thumbnail">
      <img src="{{item.src}}" alt="{{item.name}}">
      <div class="caption">
        <h3>{{item.name}}</h3>
        <p>{{item.description}}</p>
      </div>
    </div>
  </div>
</div>
```

Building Directives with Dynamic Templates

3. The markup is pretty simple and we are using the CSS classes from Bootstrap, as the generator-angm already included the Bootstrap stylesheet. Let's do the same for the video template, placing the following code in a new file and saving as `video-tpl.html`:

```html
<div>
  <iframe width="300" height="300" ng-src="{{item.src}}"
  frameborder="0" allowfullscreen></iframe>
  <h2>{{item.name}}</h2>
</div>
```

4. Now, let's add the last template for this example. Place the following code and save a new file as `text-tpl.html`:

```html
<blockquote>
  <p>{{item.src}}.</p>
  <footer>Someone famous in <cite title="Source
  Title">{{item.name}}</cite></footer>
</blockquote>
```

5. The creation process is already done, but we need to do a `$resource` service for this example. So, open the `homeService.js` that was already created by the generator, and replace it with the following code:

```js
'use strict';

/**
 * @ngdoc function
 * @name app.service:homeService
 * @description
 * # homeService
 * Service of the app
 */
angular.module('dynamic-templates')
.factory('homeService', ['$resource', function ($resource){

  var posts = [
{"type" : "image", "name" : "Black Label Society", "src" :
"https://upload.wikimedia.org/wikipedia/en/b/bd/Sonic_Brew_
Original_Cover.jpg", "description": "Lorem ipsum dolor sit amet,
consectetur adipiscing elit, sed do eiusmod tempor incididunt
ut labore et dolore magna aliqua. Ut enim ad minim veniam, quis
nostrud exercitation ullamco laboris nisi ut aliquip ex ea commodo
consequat. Duis aute irure dolor in reprehenderit in voluptate
velit esse cillum dolore eu fugiat nulla pariatur."},
{"type" : "video", "name" : "2016 Harley-Davidson
Motorcycles 883", "src" :
"http://www.youtube.com/embed/_dOxZX5gz0U"},
```

```
{"type" : "text",  "name" : "Some Text Example ", "src":
"Sample Text about crazy Motorcycles goes here."}
  ];

return {
  all: function () {
    return posts;
  }
}

}]);
```

Note that we keep the same name for the service as the generator suggested for the example code.

> On a real application, the `var post` will be a request from an endpoint API.

6. The next step is to inject the service into our controller. Let's add the following highlighted code to the `homeCtrl.js`:

```
'use strict';

/**
 * @ngdoc function
 * @name app.controller:HomeCtrl
 * @description
 * # HomeCtrl
 * Controller of the app
 */
angular.module('dynamic-templates')
.controller('HomeCtrl', ['$scope', 'homeService', '$http',
function ($scope, homeService, $http) {
  $scope.title = "Hello, Angm-Generator!";

  $scope.url = 'app/modules/shared/directives/dynamic-
  template/content.json';

  $scope.content = [];

  $scope.getContentFromFile = function() {
    $http.get($scope.url).then(function(result){
      $scope.content = result.data;
```

```
        });
      }

      $scope.getContentFromFile();

      $scope.posts = homeService.all();

    }]);
```

7. So, the last step is to add the directive markup to the `home.html` file. Open the home.html file at `app/modules/home` and add the following code:

```
<div class="row">
  <post-item class="col-lg-4" ng-repeat="item in posts"
  data="item"></post-item>
</div>
```

8. Place the previous code right after the following lines of code:

```
<div class="row">
  <content-item ng-repeat="item in content"
  content="item"></content-item>
</div>
```

9. The final result is almost the same as the previous chapter, but this way we have total control of the templates in the separated files. Open your terminal window and place the following command:

   grunt dev

Your default browser must be open and you will see a result as shown in the following picture:

How it works...

Unlike the last recipe, we used the built-in template function from AngularJS, but not the `templateUrl`. The key point here is the use of `ng-include` to inject the right template on the screen:

```
return {
  template: '<ng-include src="getTemplateUrl()"/>',
  scope: {
    item: '=data'
  },
  restrict: 'E',
}
```

Also, in this example, we are using a `controller` function and a `getTemplateUrl()` function to determine what the template must be called:

```
controller: function($scope) {
  //Pass a tpl to ng-include
  $scope.getTemplateUrl = function() {
    //We can place this piece in different services
    if ($scope.item.type == "image")
      return "app/modules/shared/directives/dynamic-
      template/image-tpl.html";
    if ($scope.item.type == "video")
      return "app/modules/shared/directives/dynamic-
      template/video-tpl.html";
    if ($scope.item.type == "text")
      return "app/modules/shared/directives/dynamic-template/text-
      tpl.html";
  }
}
```

In the previous example, we used a `switch()` function and just used `if()`. Of course, we can make use of the switch function here, but for dialectical purposes, we are keeping it a simple if statement.

Here we can note the different path for each file template, and this can be very helpful when we work on large-scale applications and in large teams.

Building Directives with Dynamic Templates

The `getTemplateurl()` function passes to `ng-include`—the URL that must be rendered on the screen. As you inspect the code on the browser, you can see the following code:

```
<ng-include src="app/modules/shared/directives/dynamic-
template/image-tpl.html" class="ng-scope"><div class="row ng-
scope">
  <div class="thumb">
    <div class="thumbnail">
      <img src="https://upload.wikimedia.org/wikipedia
      /en/b/bd/Sonic_Brew_Original_Cover.jpg" alt="Black Label
      Society">
      <div class="caption">
        <h3 class="ng-binding">Black Label Society</h3>
        <p class="ng-binding">In the early 1990s, ...</p>
      </div>
    </div>
  </div>
</div>
</ng-include>
```

And `homeCtrl.js` performs a simple get on `homeService.js` using the `$resource` features and the `all()` function:

```
$scope.posts = homeService.all();
```

You must note here the use of `http://www.youtube.com/embed/` before the video ID from YouTube. As we are working with a local server, we need to be careful with some browser/server polices, and the normal YouTube-embedded code doesn't work.

The `homeService.js` returns an `src:` property with the following video code:

```
http://www.youtube.com/embed/_dOxZX5gz0U
```

There's more...

Not all web applications have external links to pictures or videos. Often, we need to keep all content on a single server or even a single enterprise domain.

In this example, we can easily achieve this by simply replacing the video template code to use the video tag feature of HTML5.

As we can see in the following example, the `video-tpl.html` file will look like this:

```
<video controls>
  <source src="app/assets/video/01-final.ogv" type="video/ogg">
  <!--<source src="foo.mp4" type="video/mp4">-->
  Your browser does not support the <code>video</code> element.
</video>
```

To see this in action, just add the previous code to the `video-tpl.html`, right after the `iframe` tag.

Now add a `video` folder to the `assets` folder and add a video file. In our example code, we already have a file to illustrate the example.

The result will be something like the following image, an HTML5 video player with some controls:

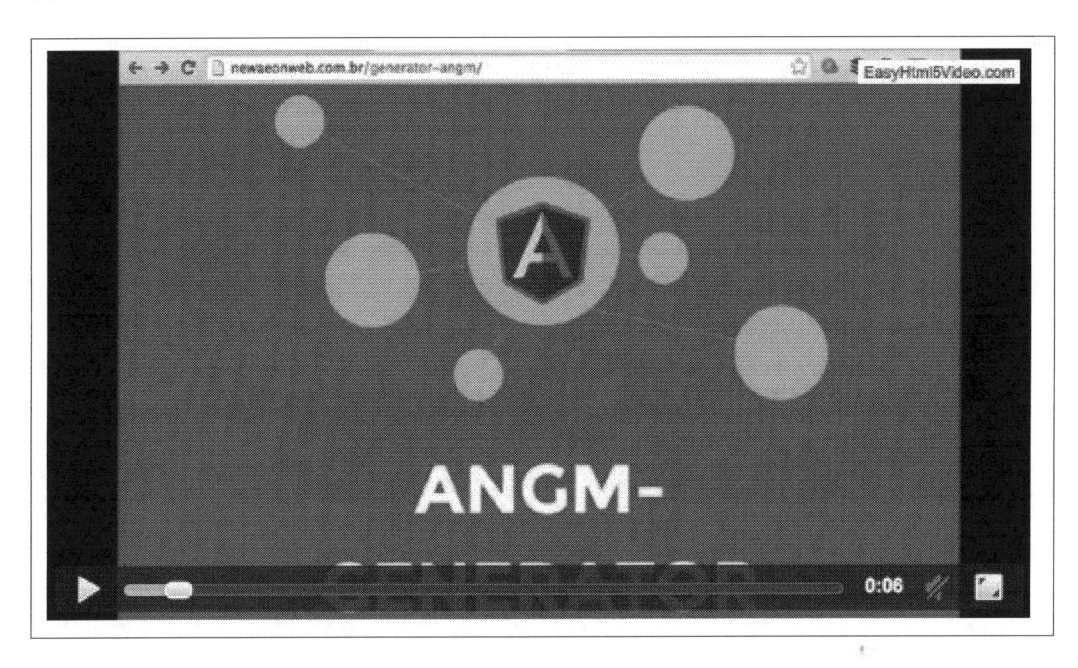

And the same technique applies to images too. Just change the template and the `src` to your own image path.

8
Creating Reusable Directives

In this chapter, we will cover:

- How to scale an AngularJS project to use reusable directives
- Building a directive as an interface component
- Creating a form directive with custom validation

Introduction

How do you scale an AngularJS project to use reusable directives? First of all we need to understand the significance of scale, and how reusable directives can impact it. Next, we need to look at some of the directives we've previously created with Bootstrap and see how we can effectively use them to accomplish our goals.

Yes, we can use an `<accordion>` directive at various points on the interface, but always within a specific context.

In the next examples, we will see how to create some directives and use them as interface components.

Creating Reusable Directives

How to scale an AngularJS project to use reusable directives

An important key is the consistency of your code; there are many ways to do it right.

Another important key is the principle of **DRY** (**Don't Repeat Yourself**). DRY code is easier to work with and will help you build applications that are more maintainable.

Pay close attention to naming conventions, this is another very important point. Using intuitive and short names makes your code easier to work and makes it easier to keep a pattern.

No pattern is absolutely failsafe or bullet proof, but you must choose which best fits your application and use it from start to finish.

Large-scale applications often grow at a steady pace from their beginning until you reach an intermediate state; however, from this stage, things tend to get out of control and grow wildly if there has been no pattern previously established since the beginning.

Let's see an example of a web interface built only with customized directives, something very similar to web components and frameworks of Polymer.

You can find more about Polymer at `https://www.polymer-project.org/1.0/`. Polymer applied the web components principle, but it is not directly related to AngularJS.

Getting ready

For the next recipe, we are still using the generator-angm. You can get the code in the examples folder at PacktPub, or open your terminal window and type:

```
yo angm
```

Name it `interface-components` and type `enter, enter, enter`.

1. Let's create some modules. Open your terminal window and type:

    ```
    yo angm:angm-module
    ```

    Name it `album` and type `enter`.

    After the command is executed, the terminal will show the files that were created:

    ```
    create app/modules/album/albumCtrl.js
    create app/modules/album/albumRoute.js
    create app/modules/album/album.html
    create app/modules/album/albumService.js
    ```

2. Create `app/modules/album/album-test.js`. Now let's rename all files to:
   - `app/modules/album/album.controller.js`
   - `app/modules/album/album.route.js`
   - `app/modules/album/album.html`
   - `app/modules/album/album.service.js`
   - `app/modules/album/album.spec.js`

3. At this stage we need to execute the Grunt task to inject all the renamed files to the `index.html` of the application. But we still need another change, this time on the `Gruntfile.js` file at the application root folder. Replace the names on the injector task and add the highlighted line:

```
injector: {
  options: {},
  local_dependencies: {
    files: {
      'index.html': [
        'bower.json',
        'app/app.js',
        'app/**/*.route.js',
        'app/**/*.controller.js',
        'app/**/*.service.js',
        'app/**/*.directive.js'
      ]
    }
  }
}
```

4. Type `grunt dev`, your default browser must be opened with the application running.

These steps are the baseline for the directives that will be created, but before we get our hands dirty, let's see an image of what we will build.

Creating Reusable Directives

Of course, we can accomplish this task using the built-in `ng-repeat` AngularJS directive with plain HTML markup. But we want to build a reusable component and don't want to repeat ourselves on each page of the application.

> You can keep the default names created using the generator-angm. We changed them here just to illustrate another name convention.

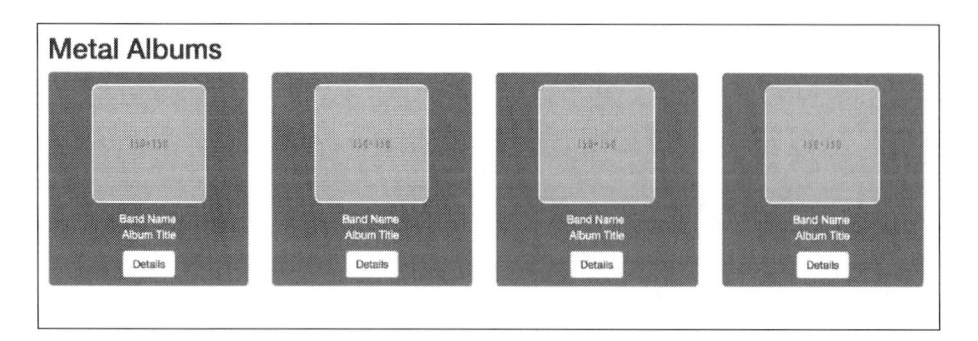

Let's replace some default code to accomplish the task.

How to do it...

1. Let's create a stylesheet at `app/assets/css` and name it `style.css`, then place the following code:

   ```
   .card {
     position: relative;
     border: 1px solid #CCC;
     border-radius: 6px;
     text-align: center;
     background-color: #D06363;
     color: #fff;
   }
   .card .album {
     position: relative;
     margin-top: 15px;
   }
   .card .album img {
     width: 150px;
     height: 150px;
     border-radius: 6%;
     border: 2px solid #fff;
   ```

```
    }
    .card .content {
        margin-top: 10px;
        padding-bottom: 10px;
    }
```

2. Now, let's add the stylesheet at the `index.html` file right after the injector tag:

   ```
   <link rel="stylesheet" href="/app/assets/css/style.css">
   ```

   The style is pretty simple and serves just for didactic purposes.

3. Inside `app/modules/shared/`, create a new folder called `directives` and add a folder in the `directives` folder, called `album-description`.

4. On `app/modules/shared/directives/album-description`, add a new file and name it `album.description.directive.js`, and place the following code:

   ```javascript
   'use strict';

   /**
    * @ngdoc function
    * @name app.directive:album-descriptionDirective
    * @description
    * # album-descriptionDirective
    * Directive of the app
    */
   angular.module('interface-components')
   .directive('albumDescription', [function () {

     return {
       restrict: 'E',
       templateUrl: 'app/modules/shared/directives/album-
         description/album.description.html',
         scope: {
           item: '='
         },
         controller: function ($scope) {
           $scope.opened = false;

           return $scope.toggle = function () {
             return $scope.opened = !$scope.opened;
           };
         }

     }

   }]);
   ```

Creating Reusable Directives

5. As we can see in the previous code, the directive uses an external HTML template, so let's create it. Place the following code in the new file and save it as `album.description.html` in the same folder as before:

```html
<div class="card">
  <div class="album">
    <img src="https://placehold.it/150x150" alt="{{
    item.band }} - {{ item.title }}" />
  </div>
  <div class="content">
    <p>{{ item.band }}<br>
    {{ item.title }}</p>
    <button type="button" class="btn btn-default" ng-
    click="toggle()">Details</button>
  </div>
  <div class="description" ng-show="opened">
    <p>{{item.description}}</p>
  </div>
</div>
```

6. The next step is to create some sample content to fill the directive. Open the `album.controller.js` at app/modules/album and replace the code with the following lines:

```js
'use strict';

/**
 * @ngdoc function
 * @name app.controller:albumCtrl
 * @description
 * # albumCtrl
 * Controller of the app
 */
angular.module('album')
.controller('AlbumCtrl', ['$scope', function ($scope) {

  $scope.listAlbums = [
    { band: "Motorhead", title: "March or Die",
    description: "Lorem ipsum dolor sit amet, consectetur
    adipiscing elit, sed do eiusmod tempor incididunt ut
    labore et dolore magna aliqua." },
    { band: "Chrome Division", title: "Infernal Eternal",
    description: "Lorem ipsum dolor sit amet, consectetur
    adipiscing elit, sed do eiusmod tempor incididunt ut
    labore et dolore magna aliqua." },
```

```
            { band: "Hellyeah", title: "Blood for Blood",
            description: "Lorem ipsum dolor sit amet, consectetur
            adipiscing elit, sed do eiusmod tempor incididunt ut
            labore et dolore magna aliqua." },
            { band: "Lynyrd Skynyrd", title: "Last of a dying
            breed", description: "Lorem ipsum dolor sit amet,
            consectetur adipiscing elit, sed do eiusmod tempor
            incididunt ut labore et dolore magna aliqua. Ut enim ad
            minim veniam, quis nostrud exercitation ullamco laboris
            nisi ut aliquip ex ea commodo consequat. Duis aute
            irure dolor in reprehenderit in voluptate velit esse
            cillum dolore eu fugiat nulla pariatur. Excepteur sint
            occaecat cupidatat non proident, sunt in culpa qui
            officia deserunt mollit anim id est laborum." }
          ]

      }]);
```

7. For this example, we insert the sample code inside the controller. In a real application, it is preferable to use a service to load this data. Now we just need to use the directive inside the `album` modules previously created in the *Getting ready* section. Open the `album.html` from `app/modules/album` and replace the code with the following lines:

```
<div class="container">
  <h1>Metal Albums</h1>
  <div class="row">
    <div class="col-sm-3" ng-repeat="album in listAlbums">
      <album-description item="album" >
      </album-description>
    </div>
  </div>
</div>
```

8. The last step is to check whether everything has gone to plan. Open your terminal on the root project folder and type `grunt dev`, you will see the result from the previous image right on your browser at the URL `http://localhost:8000/#!/album`.

Creating Reusable Directives

When we click on the **Details** button, the card opens and shows the album description as the following screenshot:

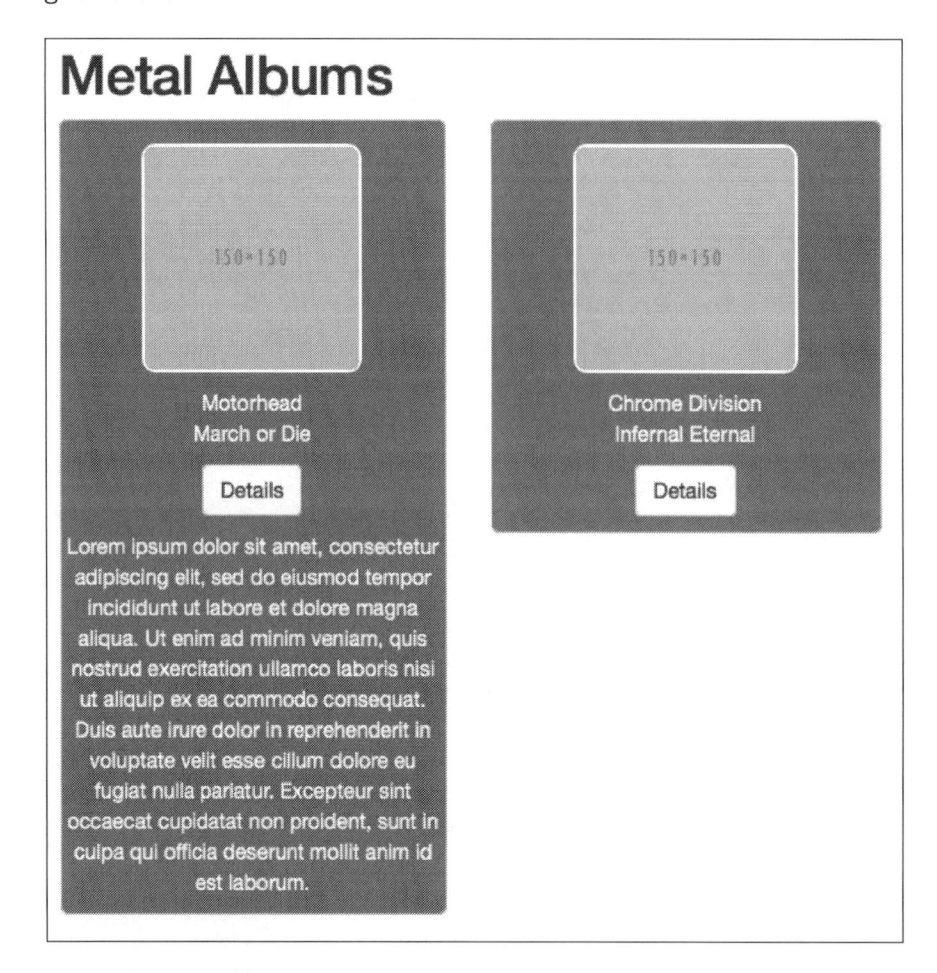

How it works...

As already mentioned, it would be very simple to write a markup in HTML and use the `ng-repeat` to build this page; however, we would need to repeat the same code on every page, therefore we would not be following the DRY principle. Instead, the directive makes the work easier. Let's see some important keys here.

In step 4, note the naming convention: we used `album-description` with a dash for the folder name, and `album.description.html` with a dot for the filename.

Using the `templateUrl: 'app/modules/shared/directives/album-description/album.description.html'` makes it very easy to customize and change the card layout, and we can also add new properties just in one file.

Using the `scope` attribute, we can isolate the code using the two-way data binding with an equals sign:

```
scope: {
  item: '='
}
```

Also, this way, our directive does not depend strictly on the code generated by the repeater:

```
<div class="col-sm-3" ng-repeat="album in listAlbums">
  <album-description item="album" >
  </album-description>
</div>
```

And we can use the directive outside the repeater anywhere on the page. For this, we need only pass the album's list name for the item owned by the directive:

```
<album-description item="listAlbums[0]" >
</album-description>
```

The controller takes care of the button collapse with more details using the built-in `ng-show` directive:

```
controller: function ($scope) {
  $scope.opened = false;

  return $scope.toggle = function () {
  return $scope.opened = !$scope.opened;
  };
}
```

Building a directive as an interface component

An important observation when we talk about directives and interface components is to understand that this is just an analogy between them, since the following doubt may arise: are not they the same thing? Not exactly.

The component is a code snippet that can be connected to any code block and still behave as expected. Even in different code blocks.

Creating Reusable Directives

A directive often receives or handles data from external sources, so for it to behave the same way, interacting with different data sources needs some adjustments.

Here, we will see a way to create a directive and encapsulate its contents to get the same result.

Getting ready

Just as we did in the previous chapters, we will continue using the same application created in the previous recipe.

In this example we will use an external library that, by itself, is already a component, a very powerful charts library called `d3.js`.

Beyond it, we will use another library called `c3.js`. In an instant, you will understand why this library helps us. For now, let's see what the official documentation says about C3.

> C3 makes it easy to generate D3-based charts by wrapping the code required to construct the entire chart. We do not need to write any more code D3. `http://c3js.org/`.

Yes, we could directly use the library D3; however, with the help of C3.js, we have a powerful wrapper on our hands.

Let's create a new module in order to use the following directive:

1. Add the following links to the `index.html` file:

   ```
   <!-- Charts Lib -->
   <script src="https://cdnjs.cloudflare.com/ajax/libs/d3/3.5.6/
   d3.min.js"></script>
   <script src="https://cdnjs.cloudflare.com/ajax/libs/c3/0.4.10/
   c3.min.js"></script>
   <!-- Charts Lib -->
   ```

2. The `scripts` tag goes right at the end of `injector:js`:

   ```
   <link rel="stylesheet"
   href="https://cdnjs.cloudflare.com/ajax/libs/c3/0.4.10/c3.m
   in.css">
   ```

3. The stylesheet goes right after the `style.css` tag. Open your terminal window at the project root and type the following command:

   yo angm:angm-module

Chapter 8

4. Name it `album-sales` and type `enter`. After the command is executed, the terminal shows the files that were created:

   ```
   create app/modules/album-sales/album-salesCtrl.js
   create app/modules/album-sales/album-salesRoute.js
   create app/modules/album-sales/album-sales.html
   create app/modules/album-sales/album-salesService.js
   create app/modules/album-sales/album-sales-test.js
   ```

5. Rename the files to the same convention used in the previous recipe:
   - app/modules/album-sales/album.sales.controller.js
   - app/modules/album-sales/album.sales.route.js
   - app/modules/album-sales/album.sales.html
   - app/modules/album-sales/album.sales.service.js
   - app/modules/album-sales/album.sales.spec.js

6. Type `grunt dev`; your default browser must be opened with the application running.
7. Check the URL `http://127.0.0.1:8000/#!/album-sales`, you will see an h1 text with Content from Album-sales Page.

How to do it...

1. Inside `app/modules/shared/directives`, create a new folder called `charts`. In `app/modules/directives/charts`, add a new file, name it `charts.directive.js`, and place the following code:

   ```
   'use strict';

   /**
    * @ngdoc function
    * @name app.directive:chartsDirective
    * @description
    * # chartsDirective
    * Directive of the app
    */
   angular.module('interface-components')
   .directive('charts', [function () {

     return {
       restrict: 'EA',
       template: '<div></div>',
       scope: {
         config: '='
   ```

147

Creating Reusable Directives

```
      },
      link: function (scope, element, attrs) {
        // Default type
        if(!scope.config.type) scope.config.type = 'line';

        //generate c3 chart data
        var chartData = scope.config;
        chartData.bindto = '#' + attrs.id;

        var chart = c3.generate(chartData);

        scope.$on("c3.resize", function(e, data) {
          chart.resize();
        });
      }

    }

  }]);
```

2. Open album.sales.html at app/modules/album-sales/album.sales.html and replace the default code with the following lines:

```
<div class="container">
  <h1>Albums Sales</h1>

  <div class="row">
    <div class="col-lg-6">
      <div class="panel panel-default panel-hovered">
        <div class="panel-heading">{{splineTitle}}</div>
        <div class="panel-body">
          <div charts id="c3-spline"
          config="splineconfig"></div>
        </div>
      </div>
    </div>
    <div class="col-lg-6">
      <div class="panel panel-default panel-hovered">
        <div class="panel-heading">{{donutTitle}}</div>
          <div class="panel-body">
            <div charts id="c3-donut"
            config="donutconfig"></div>
          </div>
      </div>
    </div>
  </div>
</div>
```

3. We are using the markup from the Twitter Bootstrap framework already included in our application due the generator, but the directive itself doesn't depend on Bootstrap. Let's add some content to the charts. Open the `album.sales.controller.js` file and replace the default code with the following lines:

```
'use strict';

/**
 * @ngdoc function
 * @name app.controller:album-salesCtrl
 * @description
 * # album-salesCtrl
 * Controller of the app
 */
angular.module('album-sales')
.controller('Album-salesCtrl', ['$scope', function
($scope){

  $scope.splineTitle = "Spline-bar";
  $scope.splineconfig = {
    data: {
      url: '/app/modules/shared/directives/charts/
      sampleContent.json',
      mimeType: 'json',
      type: "spline",
      types: {
         "Motorhead": "bar"
      }
    },
    color: {
      pattern: ["#3F51B5", "#38B4EE", "#4CAF50", "#E91E63"]
    },

    size: {
      height: 320
    }
  };

  $scope.donutTitle = "Donut";
  $scope.donutconfig = {
    data: {
      columns: [["Motorhead", 48.9], ["Chrome Division",
      17.1], ["Hellyeah", 12.9], ["Lynyrd Skynyrd", 21.1]],
      type: "donut"
    },
```

```
        size: {
          height: 320
        },
        donut: {
          width: 60
        },
        color: {
          pattern: ["#3F51B5", "#4CAF50", "#f44336", "#E91E63",
          "#38B4EE"]
        }
      }
    }]);
```

4. Now, the last step is to add the sample content at `/app/modules/shared/directives/charts/`. This is used to fill the charts with some data. Create a new file at `/app/modules/shared/directives/charts/`, save it as `sampleContent.json`, and place the following code:

```
{
  "Motorhead": [30, 100, 80, 140, 150, 200],
  "Chrome Division": [25, 100, 170, 140, 150, 50]
}
```

5. Open your terminal window at the root project folder and type:

    grunt dev

Check the following URL: `http://127.0.0.1:8000/#!/album-sales`, you will see the following image on your browser:

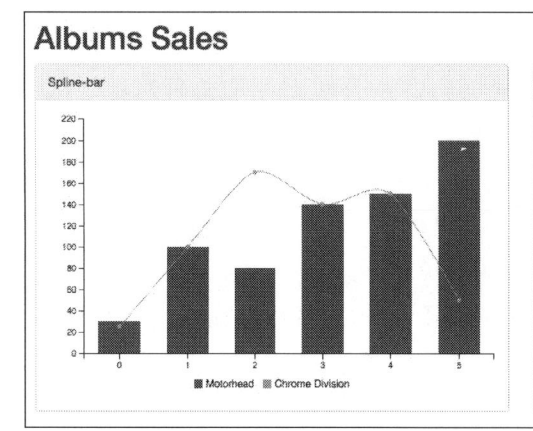

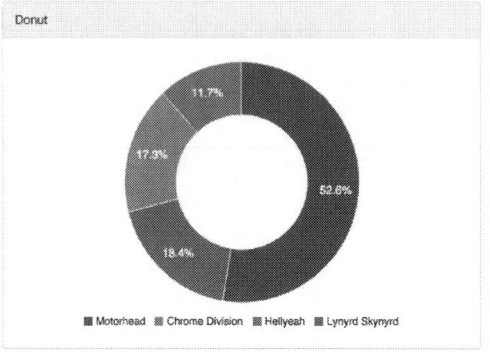

Albums Sales

Spline-bar — Motorhead, Chrome Division

Donut — Motorhead, Chrome Division, Hellyeah, Lynyrd Skynyrd (11.7%, 17.3%, 18.4%, 52.6%)

With these five steps, we have built a powerful chart directive. Contrary to what is common in other directives with external JavaScript dependence, our directive is unique. In most cases, each type of chart is determined by the name of the directive, as with `morrisjs` and `plotjs`.

In our case, the type of chart is passed as the parameter to the directive through the controller that instantiates your copy.

Let's see what happens.

How it works...

The directive has almost 34 lines of code, including comments and line breaks, but the magic happens right in the `scope` property with the two-way bindable attribute:

```
return {
  restrict: 'EA',
  template: '<div></div>',
  scope: {
    config: '='
  },
  link: function (scope, element, attrs) {
    ...
  }

}
```

The `link` function is also very simple:

```
link: function (scope, element, attrs) {
  // Default type
  if(!scope.config.type) scope.config.type = 'line';

  //generate c3 chart data
  var chartData = scope.config;
  chartData.bindto = '#' + attrs.id;

  var chart = c3.generate(chartData);

  scope.$on("c3.resize", function(e, data) {
    chart.resize();
  });
}
```

In the `if` statement, we set a default chart type as `line`. In case we are missing the chart type at the moment of creation on `album.sales.controller.js`, we just choose a line type, which should be `bar` or other.

Creating Reusable Directives

The `var chartData` will hold all the attributes passed by the `config` object from our controller.

The line `chartData.bindto = '#' + attrs.id;` grabs the ID and `c3.generate(chartData)` method to generate the chart with the `config` object.

In this case, the configuration object came from `album.sales.controller.js`, where we define: chart type, chart data, and chart pattern:

```
$scope.splineconfig = {
  data: {
    url: '/app/modules/shared/directives/charts/
    sampleContent.json',
    mimeType: 'json',
    type: "spline",
    types: {
      "Motorhead": "bar"
    }
  },
  ...
```

Also, we can pass any configuration that is available and supported by the `C3.js` library.

The markup for the charts has the attributes `config` and `id`:

```
<div charts id="c3-spline" config="splineconfig"></div>
<div charts id="c3-donut" config="donutconfig"></div>
```

The `spline` example uses an external JSON with data loaded by the Ajax built-in function inside the C3.js:

```
data: {
  url: '/app/modules/shared/directives/charts/sampleContent.json',
  mimeType: 'json',
...
```

There's more...

We can create all kinds of charts available in `C3.js` just by changing the type property directly within each controller.

Let's see an example of how this can be done.

Open the `album.sales.html` file and add the following code:

```
<div class="row">
  <div class="col-lg-6">
    <div class="panel panel-default panel-hovered">
```

```html
      <div class="panel-heading">{{lineTitle}}</div>
      <div class="panel-body">
        <div charts id="c3-line"  config="lineconfig"></div>
      </div>
    </div>
  </div>
  <div class="col-lg-6">
    <div class="panel panel-default panel-hovered">
      <div class="panel-heading">{{pieTitle}}</div>
      <div class="panel-body">
        <div charts id="c3-pie" config="pieconfig"></div>
      </div>
    </div>
  </div>
</div>

<div class="row">
  <div class="col-lg-6">
    <div class="panel panel-default panel-hovered">
      <div class="panel-heading">{{barTitle}}</div>
      <div class="panel-body">
        <div charts id="c3-bar" config="barconfig"></div>
      </div>
    </div>
  </div>
  <div class="col-lg-6">
    <div class="panel panel-default panel-hovered">
      <div class="panel-heading">{{stackedbarTitle}}</div>
      <div class="panel-body">
        <div charts id="c3-stackedbar"
        config="stackedbarconfig"></div>
      </div>
    </div>
  </div>
</div>
```

Add the following code to `album.sales.controller.js`:

```javascript
// Charts// Line Chart
$scope.lineTitle = "Line";
$scope.lineconfig = {
  data: {
    columns: [
      ['Hellyeah', 30, 200, 100, 200, 150, 250],
      ['Lynyrd Skynyrd', 50, 20, 10, 40, 15, 25]
```

Creating Reusable Directives

```
      ]
    }
  };

  // Bar Chart
  $scope.barTitle = "Bar";
  $scope.barconfig = {
    data: {
      columns: [
        ['Hellyeah', 30, 200, 100, 400, 150, 250],
        ['Lynyrd Skynyrd', 130, 100, 140, 200, 150, 50]
      ],
      type: 'bar',
      onclick: function (d, element) {
        alert('yeah ' + JSON.stringify(d));
      }
    },
    bar: {
      width: {
        ratio: 0.5 // this makes bar width 50% of length between ticks
      }
      // or
      //width: 100 // this makes bar width 100px
    }
  };

  // Stacked Bar Chart
  $scope.stackedbarTitle = "Stacked Bar";
  $scope.stackedbarconfig = {
    data: {
      columns: [
        ['Motorhead', -30, 200, 200, 400, -150, 250],
        ['Chrome Division', 130, 100, -100, 200, -150, 50],
        ['Hellyeah', -230, 200, 200, -300, 250, 250]
      ],
      type: 'bar',
      groups: [
        ['data1', 'data2']
      ]
    },
```

```
      grid: {
        y: {
          lines: [{value:0}]
        }
      }
    };


    // Pie Chart
    $scope.pieTitle = "Pie";
    $scope.pieconfig = {
      data: {
        columns: [
          ["Motorhead", 0.2, 0.2, 0.2, 0.2, 0.2, 0.4, 0.3, 0.2, 0.2,
          0.1, 0.2, 0.2, 0.1, 0.1, 0.2, 0.4, 0.4, 0.3, 0.3, 0.3, 0.2,
          0.4, 0.2, 0.5, 0.2, 0.2, 0.4, 0.2, 0.2, 0.2, 0.2, 0.4, 0.1,
          0.2, 0.2, 0.2, 0.2, 0.1, 0.2, 0.2, 0.3, 0.3, 0.2, 0.6, 0.4,
          0.3, 0.2, 0.2, 0.2, 0.2],
           ["Chrome Division", 1.4, 1.5, 1.5, 1.3, 1.5, 1.3, 1.6, 1.0,
          1.3, 1.4, 1.0, 1.5, 1.0, 1.4, 1.3, 1.4, 1.5, 1.0, 1.5, 1.1,
          1.8, 1.3, 1.5, 1.2, 1.3, 1.4, 1.4, 1.7, 1.5, 1.0, 1.1, 1.0,
          1.2, 1.6, 1.5, 1.6, 1.5, 1.3, 1.3, 1.3, 1.2, 1.4, 1.2, 1.0,
          1.3, 1.2, 1.3, 1.3, 1.1, 1.3],
           ["Hellyeah", 2.5, 1.9, 2.1, 1.8, 2.2, 2.1, 1.7, 1.8, 1.8,
          2.5, 2.0, 1.9, 2.1, 2.0, 2.4, 2.3, 1.8, 2.2, 2.3, 1.5, 2.3,
          2.0, 2.0, 1.8, 2.1, 1.8, 1.8, 1.8, 2.1, 1.6, 1.9, 2.0, 2.2,
          1.5, 1.4, 2.3, 2.4, 1.8, 1.8, 2.1, 2.4, 2.3, 1.9, 2.3, 2.5,
          2.3, 1.9, 2.0, 2.3, 1.8],
        ],
        type: "pie"
      }
    };
```

Now type the `grunt dev` command at your terminal and check:
http://127.0.0.1:8000/#!/album-sales.

Creating Reusable Directives

The result will be similar to the following screenshot:

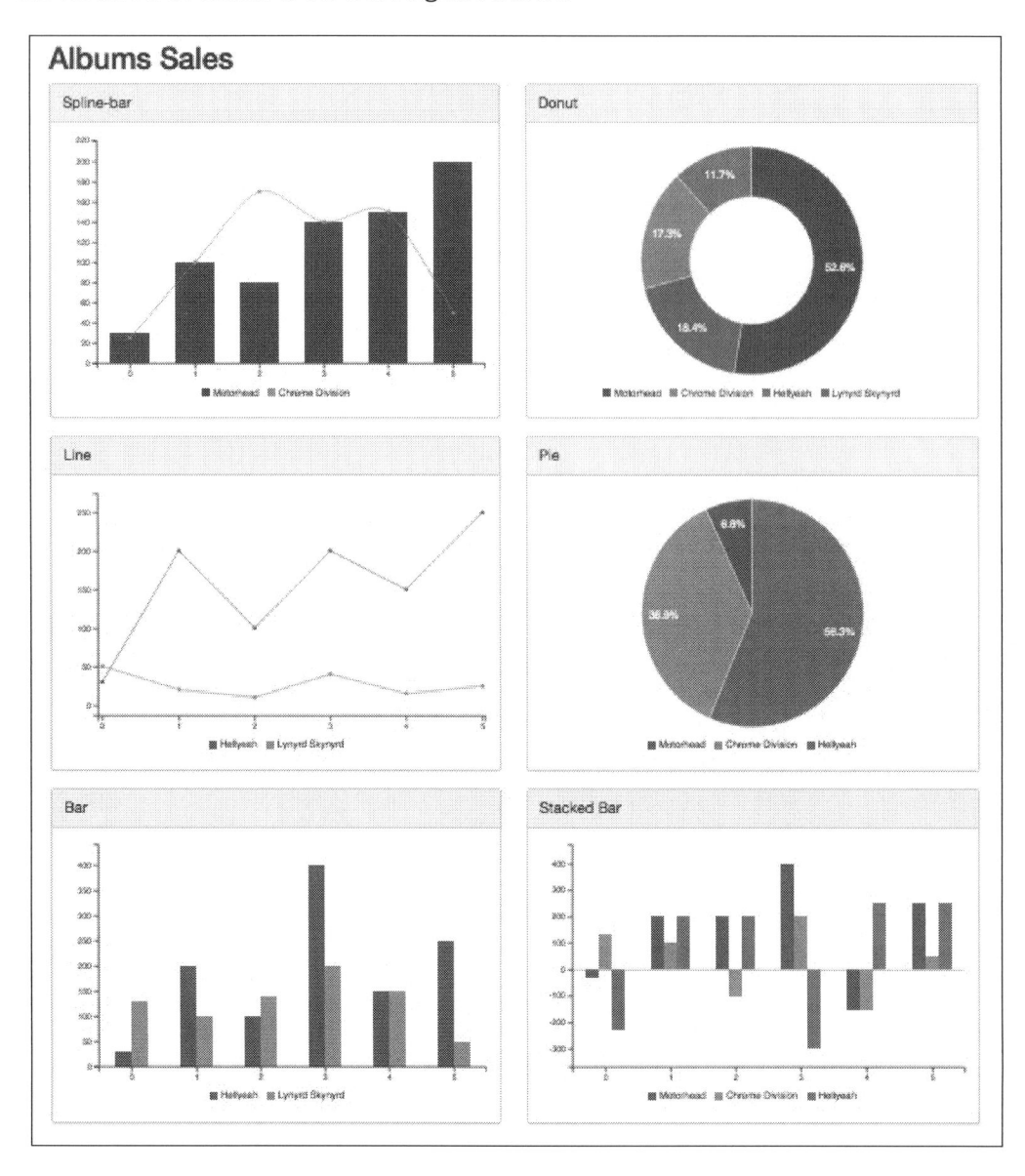

We have six types of charts using the same directive markup:

```
<div charts id="c3-spline" config="splineconfig"></div>
<div charts id="c3-donut" config="donutconfig"></div>
<div charts id="c3-line"   config="lineconfig"></div>
<div charts id="c3-pie" config="pieconfig"></div>
<div charts id="c3-bar" config="barconfig"></div>
<div charts id="c3-stackedbar" config="stackedbarconfig"></div>
```

See also

- You can find all configuration possibilities at the C3.js reference manual at http://c3js.org/reference.html

Creating a form directive with custom validation

Continuing within the context of the previous examples, we will now create a custom directive to validate some form fields. This recipe applies to any type of form field; however, we will use the <select> tag.

AngularJS offers some very useful resources for form validation with built-in directives. We will create a component that can be reused elsewhere in our application.

Getting ready

Just as we did in the previous chapters, we will continue using the same application created in the previous recipe.

In this example, we will use an external library called ngMessages.

For the purpose of this example, we just add the library as a dependency in our index.html, using a **Content Delivery Network** (**CDN**), as we did in the previous recipe.

Add the following link to the index.html file:

```
<!-- Ng Messages-->
<script src="https://cdnjs.cloudflare.com/ajax/libs/angular.js/1.4.5/angular-messages.min.js"></script>
<!-- Ng Messages-->
```

The scripts tag goes right at the end of <!-- Charts Lib -->.

Creating Reusable Directives

Now add the `ngMessages` at the end of `app.js` in the app folder as shown in the following highlighted code:

```
angular.module('interface-components', [
  'ngResource',
  'ui.bootstrap',
  'ngCookies',
  'ngAnimate',
  'ngTouch',
  'ngSanitize',
  'ui.router',
  'album',
  'album-sales',
  'ngMessages'
])
```

How to do it...

1. Create a new folder on `app/modules/shared/directive` and name it `album-rating`. Create a new file and place the following code. Save the file as `album.rating.directive.js`:

    ```
    'use strict';

    /**
     * @ngdoc function
     * @name app.directive:albumRatingDirective
     * @description
     * # albumRatingDirective
     * Directive of the app
     */
    angular.module('interface-components')
      .directive('albumRating', [function () {

        return {
          restrict: 'E',
          require: '?ngModel',
          templateUrl: 'app/modules/shared/directives/album-
          rating/album.rating.html',
          link: function(scope, element, attrs, ngModel) {
            if (!ngModel) return;

            // Copy from ngModel and place on local scope
            ngModel.$render = function() {
              scope.item = {
    ```

```
          music: ngModel.$viewValue,
          album: ngModel.$viewValue
      };
};

// Init score selects
scope.selects = {

  music: function() {

    // Set score
    var score = 10;

    var musicScore = [];

    // Simple for statement to generate scores
    for (var i = 1; i <= score; i++) {
      var toString = i.toString();
        // Simple number format adding 0 for single
        number
        musicScore.push((toString.length < 2) ? '0' +
        toString : toString);
    }

    return musicScore;
  },
  albums: function() {
    var albumsList = ['March or Die', 'Aces of Spades',
    'Iron Fist'];

    return albumsList;
  }
};
// Listen for chnages
scope.$watch('item', function(item) {
  // Mandatory filds
    if (attrs.required) {

      var albumIsValid = !!item.album;
      var musicIsValid = !!item.music;
      // Validation
      ngModel.$setValidity('required', albumIsValid ||
      musicIsValid ? true : false);
      ngModel.$setValidity('albumRequired',
      albumIsValid ? true : false);
```

Creating Reusable Directives

```
              ngModel.$setValidity('musicRequired',
              musicIsValid ? true : false);

              // ngModel update
              if (albumIsValid && musicIsValid) {
                ngModel.$setViewValue('Best Album: ' +
                item.album + ' ,Music rating: ' + item.music +
                ' Stars');
              }
            }
          }, true);
        }
      }
    }]);
```

2. Create a new file and place the following code, save the file as `album.rating.html`:

```html
<div class="row">
  <div class="col-sm-4">
    Best Album
    <select ng-model="item.album" ng-options="i for i in
    selects.albums()" class="form-control">
      <option value="" disabled>----</option>
    </select>
  </div>
  <div class="col-sm-4">
    Music
    <select ng-model="item.music" ng-options="i for i in
    selects.music()" class="form-control">
      <option value="" disabled>--</option>
    </select>
  </div>
</div>
```

3. Let's use the same `album.html` page and place the following code right after the `album-description` tag:

```html
<br>
<form name="bandForm" novalidate>
  <album-rating name="album" ng-model="user.choices"
  required></album-rating>
  <hr>
  <alert  type="danger" ng-if="bandForm.$invalid">
    <ul ng-messages="bandForm.album.$error" ng-messages-
    multiple>
```

```
        <li ng-message="albumRequired">Please Choose an
        Album</li>
        <li ng-message="musicRequired">Please Rating the
        music</li>
      </ul>
    </alert>
  </form>
  <div ng-hide="bandForm.$invalid" class="well">
    {{ user.choices }}
  </div>
```

4. Add the following code to the `album.html` page, right after the album description directive:

```
<br>
<form name="bandForm" novalidate>
  <album-rating name="album" ng-model="user.choices"
  required></album-rating>
  <hr>
  <alert  type="danger" ng-if="bandForm.$invalid">
    <ul ng-messages="bandForm.album.$error" ng-messages-
    multiple>
        <li ng-message="albumRequired">Please Choose an
        Album</li>
        <li ng-message="musicRequired">Please Rating the
        music</li>
      </ul>
    </alert>
  </form>
  <div ng-hide="bandForm.$invalid" class="well">
    {{ user.choices }}
    </div>
```

5. Open your terminal window at the root project folder and type:

   grunt dev

Creating Reusable Directives

Check the URL `http://127.0.0.1:8000/#!/album`. You will see the following image on your browser:

When we choose an album and a score, the result will be the same as the following screenshot:

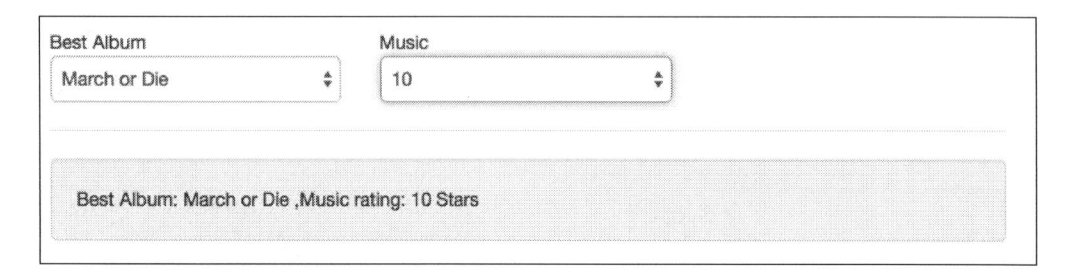

How it works...

Now, let's understand what happened with the directive. You noticed that this time we did not use any code in an external controller. This directive was composed using only the property `link()` function.

Also, we used the `ngModel`:

```
// Copy from ngModel and place on local scope
ngModel.$render = function() {
  scope.item = {
    music: ngModel.$viewValue,
    album: ngModel.$viewValue
  };
};
```

> Let's see what the official documentation says about ngModel: The
> ngModel directive binds an input, select, textarea (or custom form control)
> to a property on the scope using NgModelController, which is created
> and exposed by this directive.
>
> NgModel is responsible for:
>
> - Binding the view into the model, which other directives, such as input, textarea, or select, require
> - Providing validation behavior (for example, required, number, email, url)
> - Keeping the state of the control (valid/invalid, dirty/pristine, touched/untouched, validation errors)
> - Setting related CSS classes on the element (ng-valid, ng-invalid, ng-dirty, ng-pristine, ng-touched, ng-untouched, ng-empty, ng-not-empty), including animations
> - Registering the control with its parent form

This way, we can map the alterations that come into our select tag within the template of the directive:

```
<select ng-model="item.album" ng-options="i for i in
selects.albums()" class="form-control">
  <option value="" disabled>----</option>
</select>
<select ng-model="item.music" ng-options="i for i in
selects.music()" class="form-control">
  <option value="" disabled>--</option>
</select>
```

The ng-repeat runs over the scope.selects function inside the link function, where we return two functions:

```
scope.selects = {

  music: function() {
    ...
  },
  albums: function() {
    ...
  }
;
```

Chapter 8

163

Creating Reusable Directives

And for every alteration that the model receives, the `watch()` function applies validation and sets the values chosen in the `select` box:

```
scope.$watch('item', function(item) {
  // Mandatory fields
  if (attrs.required) {

    var albumIsValid = !!item.album;
    var musicIsValid = !!item.music;

    // Validation
    ngModel.$setValidity('required', albumIsValid || musicIsValid
    ? true : false);
    ngModel.$setValidity('albumRequired', albumIsValid ? true :
    false);
    ngModel.$setValidity('musicRequired', musicIsValid ? true :
    false);

    // ngModel update
    if (albumIsValid && musicIsValid) {
      ngModel.$setViewValue('Best Album: ' + item.album + ' ,Music
      rating: ' + item.music + ' Stars');
    }
  }
}, true);
```

The `album.html` file uses the directive and the `ngMessages` validation to show some warning before the form can be completed.

In this recipe, we try to show how it is possible to combine some built-in directives within a custom form component directive using AngularJS resources, in order to help us complete a task.

See also

- More information about `ngModel` can be found at https://docs.angularjs.org/api/ng/directive/ngModel, and more about `ngMessages` can be found at https://docs.angularjs.org/api/ngMessages/directive/ngMessages

9
Directive Unit Testing with Karma and Jasmine

In this chapter, we will cover:

- How to test AngularJS apps using Karma and Karma Runner
- Writing tests for directives with Jasmine
- Testing elements when the scope changes

Introduction

As we already know, AngularJS is designed to be fully testable. Its engineers built the framework in such a way that it is possible to test everything: controllers, services, and of course, custom directives.

In this chapter, we will follow some recipes to make your job easier when it is necessary to test your own directives.

At first glance, it may seem difficult to test custom directives, but actually there are some steps we can take to facilitate this.

Some tools help us in this task, among them there is one in particular that makes it even easier.

It is a very popular IDE among JavaScript developers, known as **WebStorm**.

Directive Unit Testing with Karma and Jasmine

We will show you how to configure the IDE and use the Karma Test Runner, but you can follow the next examples using the same editor that was used on the previous examples.

> You can download the trial version at: `https://www.jetbrains.com/webstorm/`.

How to test AngularJS apps using Karma and Karma Runner

Before we dive deep into custom directives testing, let's see how to configure and use the WebStorm. But first, let's build the baseline code for the next recipes.

Getting ready

As usual, we are still using the generator-angm to build the baseline code.

1. Create a new folder and name it `directive-unit-testing`. Open your terminal window and type:

    ```
    yo angm
    ```

2. Type `directive-unit-testing` and press *Enter, Enter, Enter*. At the end of the command, we can see all the versions installed; you will note that we are using the last stable version from AngularJS at the time of writing:

    ```
    bower install          json3#3.3.1
    bower install          es5-shim#3.1.0
    bower install          bootstrap#3.3.5
    bower install          angular-resource#1.4.7
    bower install          angular-bootstrap#0.11.2
    bower install          angular-ui-router#0.2.15
    bower install          jquery#2.1.4
    bower install          angular#1.4.7
    bower install          angular-route#1.4.7
    bower install          angular-cookies#1.4.7
    bower install          angular-touch#1.4.7
    bower install          angular-animate#1.4.7
    bower install          angular-mocks#1.4.7
    bower install          angular-sanitize#1.4.7
    ```

Chapter 9

At this moment, we have the baseline to understand how Karma works. Let's see how to configure the IDE for tests with Karma Runner.

How to do it...

1. Open the WebStorm IDE. On the welcome screen, choose the open folder option and select the folder you have just created, `directive-unit-testing`.

2. After all project files are indexed by the IDE, we can keep going and set up the Karma Runner. On the WebStorm menu, click on **Run** | **Edit Configurations** and you will see the following screenshot:

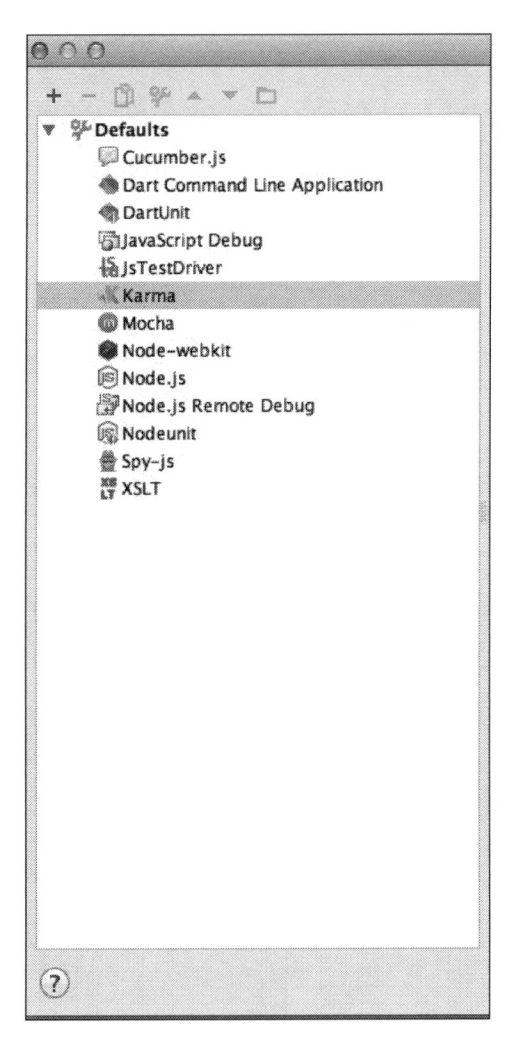

Directive Unit Testing with Karma and Jasmine

3. You may notice that WebStorm has a range of engines for testing that can be seen on the previous image. Press the plus sign in the top-left corner and fill in the fields at the right-hand side, as in the following screenshot:

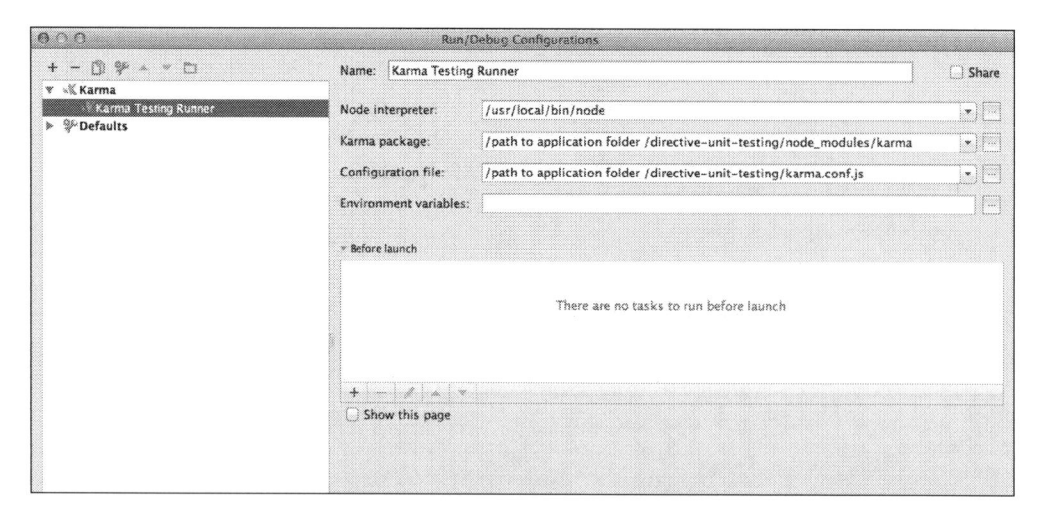

> Note that the path to the application folder must be replaced with your own path to the `directive-unit-testing` folder for the Karma package and Configuration file. Another important point is that we already have the `Karma.conf.js` file due to generator-angm.

- **Node Interpreter**: You will see the path to your local Node installation (on Mac OS X this is `usr/local/bin/node`) in this field.
- **Karma Package**: You will see the path to the Karma folder inside the `node_modules` folder in the root application folder in this field.
- **Configuration file**: You will see the path to the `Karma.conf.js` file inside the root application folder in this field. Click on **Apply** and then on the **OK** button. After that, we can see at the top of WebStorm our test runner configured and ready to use, as seen in the following screenshot:

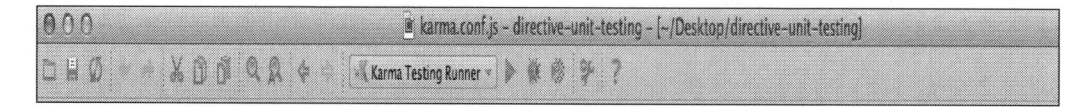

4. Now we just need to press the Play button at the right-hand side of the Karma Test Runner. On the bottom of the IDE we can see the testing tab running the tests:

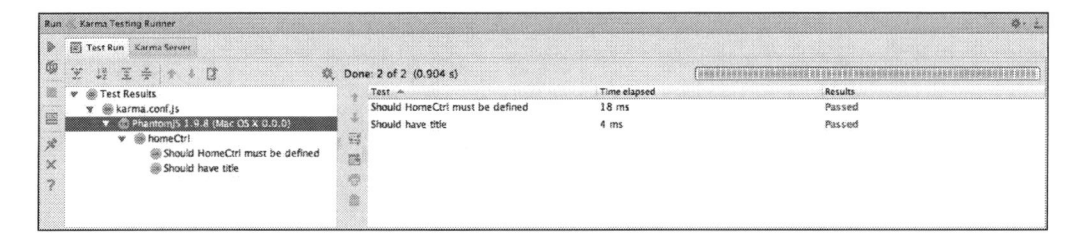

The preceding screenshot shows us the tests that were run and to which files the tests refer. We also have the runtime and the test result: green if passed and red if failed.

How it works...

By default, WebStorm already has the Karma Runner, so we just need to configure it. In fact, the generator we use already has some preconfigured testing libraries, as we can see in the `package.json` file at the application root folder:

```
"karma": "~0.12.0",
"karma-chrome-launcher": "~0.1.2",
"karma-coverage": "~0.2.0",
"karma-firefox-launcher": "~0.1.3",
"karma-jasmine": "~0.2.1",
"karma-phantomjs-launcher": "~0.1.2"
```

As we can see in the previous screenshot, you can click on the title of the test on the left pane and the WebStorm IDE automatically directs you to the file in which the test was written.

This is an extremely important feature when dealing with many test files per module. In this case, we found the following file at `app/modules/home/home-test.js file`. Don't worry about the syntax, in the next recipe we will dive deep into Jasmine and the test syntax for directives:

```
'use strict';

(function () {
  describe('homeCtrl', function () {
    var controller = null, $scope = null;

    beforeEach(function () {
      module('directive-unit-testing');
```

Directive Unit Testing with Karma and Jasmine

```
    });

    beforeEach(inject(function ($controller, $rootScope) {
      $scope = $rootScope.$new();
      controller = $controller('HomeCtrl', {
        $scope: $scope
      });
    }));

    it('Should HomeCtrl must be defined', function () {
      expect(controller).toBeDefined();
    });

    it('Should have title', function() {
    expect($scope.title).toBe('Hello, Angm-Generator!');

    });

  });
})();
```

One of the most important steps here was done by the generator-angm, the `Karma.conf.js` file with the following configuration. The file is fully commented in order to form a better understanding:

```
'use strict';

// Karma configuration
module.exports = function(config) {
  config.set({
    // Frameworks to use
    frameworks: ['jasmine'],

    // List of files / patterns to load in the browser
    files: [
      src/bower_components/jquery/dist/jquery.js',
      'src/bower_components/es5-shim/es5-shim.js',
      'src/bower_components/json3/lib/json3.min.js',
      'src/bower_components/bootstrap/dist/js/bootstrap.js',
      'src/bower_components/angular/angular.js',
      'src/bower_components/angular-resource/angular-resource.js',
      'src/bower_components/angular-mocks/angular-mocks.js',
      'src/bower_components/angular-cookies/angular-cookies.js',
      'src/bower_components/angular-sanitize/angular-sanitize.js',
      'src/bower_components/angular-animate/angular-animate.js',
      'src/bower_components/angular-touch/angular-touch.js',
```

```
      'src/bower_components/angular-route/angular-route.js',
      'src/bower_components/angular-ui-router/release/angular-ui-
      router.js',
      'src/bower_components/angular-bootstrap/ui-bootstrap-
      tpls.js',
      'app/app.js',
      'app/modules/home/homeCtrl.js',
      'app/modules/home/homeRoute.js',
      'app/modules/home/home-test.js',
      'app/modules/**/*Ctrl.js',
      'app/modules/**/*Route.js',
      'app/modules/**/*Service.js',
      'app/modules/**/*-test.js'
    ],

    // Test results reporter to use
    // Possible values: 'dots', 'progress', 'junit', 'growl',
    'coverage'
    //reporters: ['progress'],
    reporters: ['progress'],

    // Web server port
    port: 9876,

    // Enable / disable colors in the output (reporters and logs)
    colors: true,

    // Level of logging
    // Possible values: config.LOG_DISABLE || config.LOG_ERROR ||
    config.LOG_WARN || config.LOG_INFO || config.LOG_DEBUG
    logLevel: config.LOG_INFO,

    // Enable / disable watching file and executing tests whenever
    any file changes
    autoWatch: true,

    // Start these browsers, currently available:
    // - Chrome
    // - ChromeCanary
    // - Firefox
    // - Opera
    // - Safari (only Mac)
    // - PhantomJS
    // - IE (only Windows)
    browsers: ['PhantomJS'],
```

Directive Unit Testing with Karma and Jasmine

```
        // If browser does not capture in given timeout [ms], kill it
        captureTimeout: 60000,

        // Continuous Integration mode
        // If true, it capture browsers, run tests and exit
        singleRun: true
    });
};
```

Almost all AngularJS generators have the Karma and Karma Runner preconfigured.

If you started your project from scratch, you just need to install Karma and Karma Runner manually.

There's more...

In the previous example, we used a powerful IDE for developing applications with AngularJS, however any text editor can be used for this purpose, as well as tests that can be performed from the command line.

Let's see how to perform the tests using the terminal. Open your terminal window at the root folder of `directive-unit-testing` and type:

npm test

You can see the final output on your terminal, as follows:

```
> karma start karma.conf.js

INFO [karma]: Karma v0.12.37 server started at http://localhost:9876/
INFO [launcher]: Starting browser PhantomJS
INFO [PhantomJS 1.9.8 (Mac OS X 0.0.0)]: Connected on socket yy7B-hr6lSftShuxmRHF with id 40428767
LOG: 'AngularJS run() function...'
LOG: 'AngularJS run() function...'
PhantomJS 1.9.8 (Mac OS X 0.0.0): Executed 2 of 2 SUCCESS (0.002 secs / 0.023 secs)
```

This is possible because the `package.json` file has this command preconfigured by the generator we are using.

Another important point we need to note is that Karma enables us to run tests using the browser. For this, we must replace the following highlighted line in the browser you want to use:

```
    // Start these browsers, currently available:
    //  - Chrome
    //  - ChromeCanary
    //  - Firefox
    //  - Opera
    //  - Safari (only Mac)
```

```
// - PhantomJS
// - IE (only Windows)
browsers: ['PhantomJS'],
```

In this case, we are using PhantomJS, a headless Webkit engine built with JavaScript and featuring a huge API to support many web standards such as JSON, CSS selectors, and many more.

> Note that you need to have the browser pre-installed on your machine, moreover you must install the launcher of the chosen browser.

See also

- You can read more about Karma at: `http://karma-runner.github.io/0.13/intro/how-it-works.html`
- More info about PhantomJS can be found at `http://phantomjs.org/`

Writing tests for directives with Jasmine

As we commented in the previous chapter, we use the Jasmine framework for writing tests. Let's take a look at what the official documentation says about Jasmine.

> Jasmine is a behavior-driven development framework for testing JavaScript code. It does not depend on any other JavaScript frameworks. It does not require the DOM. And it has a clean, obvious syntax so that you can easily write tests.

Getting ready

For the next recipe we use a code base that was previously created in *Chapter 8*, *Creating Reusable Directives*, which charts the directive with some minor changes.

You can download the code from the `Chapter 8` folder directly from the Packt Publishing website, or by following the steps using this chapter's sample code.

Remember that in our previous example, we focused only on configuring the application to perform the test with Karma and Karma Runner.

Directive Unit Testing with Karma and Jasmine

Before we start writing our code, it's important to remember that the directives are used to manipulate the DOM in AngularJS applications, unlike controllers or services, where directives manipulate the DOM through the use of HTML templates.

Let's see the necessary steps to get the baseline code for the next recipes:

1. Grab the source code from the `Chapter 8` folder.
2. Open the `index.html` file at the application root and replace the CDN script links at the bottom of the file, with the following links:

   ```
   <!-- Charts Lib -->
   <script src="/app/modules/shared/directives/charts/d3.min.js"></script>
   <script src="/app/modules/shared/directives/charts/c3.min.js"></script>
   <!-- Charts Lib -->
   ```

3. You can grab the content from both files at their URLs. And as you can see, we created two new files in the `/app/modules/shared/directives/charts/` folder, one for `d3.min.js` and another for `c3.min.js`.

> Step 3 is pretty important because `karma.conf.js` needs files on your local machine, not on any CDN, to run the tests properly.

4. Now we need to edit the `karma.conf.js` file. Let's replace the following highlighted code:

   ```
   'use strict';

   // Karma configuration
   module.exports = function(config) {
     config.set({
       // Frameworks to use
       frameworks: ['jasmine'],

       // List of files / patterns to load in the browser
       files: [
         'src/bower_components/jquery/dist/jquery.js',
         'src/bower_components/es5-shim/es5-shim.js',
         'src/bower_components/json3/lib/json3.min.js',
         'src/bower_components/bootstrap/dist/js/bootstrap.js',
         'src/bower_components/angular/angular.js',
         'src/bower_components/angular-resource/angular-resource.js',
   ```

```
            'src/bower_components/angular-mocks/angular-
            mocks.js',
            'src/bower_components/angular-cookies/angular-
            cookies.js',
            'src/bower_components/angular-sanitize/angular-
            sanitize.js',
            'src/bower_components/angular-animate/angular-
            animate.js',
            'src/bower_components/angular-touch/angular-
            touch.js',
            'src/bower_components/angular-route/angular-
            route.js',
            'src/bower_components/angular-ui-
            router/release/angular-ui-router.js',
            'src/bower_components/angular-bootstrap/ui-bootstrap-
            tpls.js',
            'app/app.js',
            'app/modules/home/home.controller.js',
            'app/modules/home/home.route.js',
            'app/modules/home/home.spec.js',
            'app/modules/**/*.controller.js',
            'app/modules/**/*.route.js',
            'app/modules/**/*.service.js',
             'app/modules/**/*.directive.js',
            'app/modules/**/*.spec.js',

             'app/modules/shared/directives/charts/d3.min.js',
             'app/modules/shared/directives/charts/c3.min.js'
        ],

        // Test results reporter to use
        // Possible values: 'dots', 'progress', 'junit',
        'growl', 'coverage'
        //reporters: ['progress'],
        reporters: ['progress'],

        // Web server port
        port: 9876,

        // Enable / disable colors in the output (reporters and
        logs)
        colors: true,
```

Directive Unit Testing with Karma and Jasmine

```
        // Level of logging
        // Possible values: config.LOG_DISABLE ||
        config.LOG_ERROR || config.LOG_WARN || config.LOG_INFO
        || config.LOG_DEBUG
        logLevel: config.LOG_INFO,

        // Enable / disable watching file and executing tests
        whenever any file changes
        autoWatch: true,

        // Start these browsers, currently available:
        // - Chrome
        // - ChromeCanary
        // - Firefox
        // - Opera
        // - Safari (only Mac)
        // - PhantomJS
        // - IE (only Windows)
        browsers: ['PhantomJS'],

        // If browser does not capture in given timeout [ms],
        kill it
        captureTimeout: 60000,

        // Continuous Integration mode
        // If true, it capture browsers, run tests and exit
        singleRun: true
    });
};
```

The previous change puts all application dependencies within the naming convention that we adopted previously.

Now we have all the code prepared, let's create our directive test.

How to do it...

1. Let's add a new file to the charts directive folder at `app/modules/shared/directives/charts/`, and save it as `charts.spec.js`.

2. Place the following code in the charts.spec.js file:

```
'use strict';

(function() {
    describe('chart directive test', function() {
```

```javascript
//Variables used on tests
var $scope, elem, iSo;

//load the app module and all dependencies
beforeEach(function () {
  module('interface-components');
});

beforeEach(inject(function ($rootScope, $compile) {
  $scope = $rootScope.$new();
  //Simulate Data to fill Directive
  $scope.config = {
    data: {
      columns: [["Motorhead", 48.9], ["Chrome
      Division", 16.1], ["Hellyeah", 10.9], ["Lynyrd
      Skynyrd", 17.1]]
    },
    size: {
      height: 320
    },
    donut: {
      width: 60
    },
    color: {
      pattern: ["#3F51B5", "#4CAF50", "#f44336",
      "#E91E63", "#38B4EE"]
    }
  };
  // Emulate the Directive itself
  elem = '<div charts id="c3-donut"
  config="config"></div>';

  //complile element
  elem = $compile(elem)($scope);

  //digest the scope to register the elem
  $scope.$digest();
  iSo = elem.isolateScope();

}));

// Create an Object
it('should using isolate scope', function() {
  expect(iSo).toBeDefined('object');
});
```

Directive Unit Testing with Karma and Jasmine

```
      // Create an object
      it('should create a config object with iSo scope',
      function() {
        expect(iSo.config).toBeDefined('object');
      });
    });
  })();
```

3. Now that we have just created the test, we need to verify that all assertions will pass successfully.

   Go back to the WebStorm IDE and run the tests by clicking the play button, which is next to our test runner, as shown in the following screenshot:

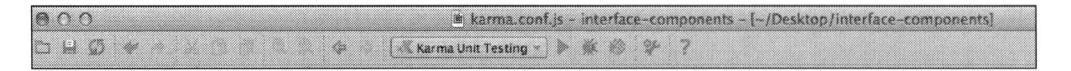

Maybe you need to reconfigure the Karma Runner. For this, follow steps 1 to 4 of the first recipe.

As we saw in the previous recipe, we will see the testing result at the bottom panel on WebStorm, as in the following screenshot:

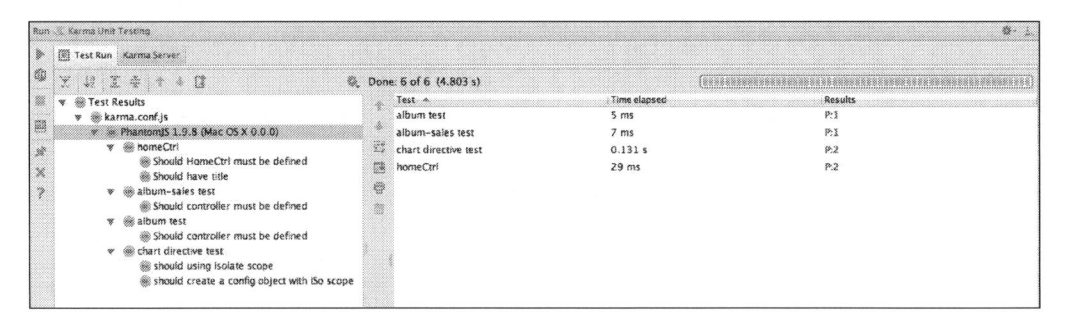

In the preceding screenshot, we can see that the tests passed with success.

In the left panel, you can see all the tests that were executed, all with a green icon. On the right, we have the test name and the running time.

How it works...

The test writing syntax came from the Jasmine framework, determined on the `karma.conf.js` file:

```
config.set({
  // Frameworks to use
  frameworks: ['jasmine'],
  ...
)}
```

This line determines which framework will be used, the possible values are: `['jasmine']`, `['mocha']` or `['qunit']`. All are pretty similar, just with different syntax.

So, the `describe()` function is common between all frameworks, the first parameter is the test name, and the second is a function:

```
describe('chart directive test', function() {...}
```

To start the tests, we need to load the application, so we are using the: `beforeEach()` function:

```
beforeEach(function () {
  module('interface-components');
});
```

And to create and emulate the data and the directive itself, we are using the `beforeEach()` function, this time injecting `$rootScope` and `$compile`:

```
beforeEach(inject(function ($rootScope, $compile) {...}
```

We need `$compile` to render the directive. Remember the directive manipulates the DOM with templates:

```
// Emulate the Directive itself
elem = '<div charts id="c3-donut" config="config"></div>';

//compile element
elem = $compile(elem)($scope);

//digest the scope to register the elem
$scope.$digest();

iSo = elem.isolateScope();
```

Directive Unit Testing with Karma and Jasmine

And last but not least, there is `isolateScope()`. As we have seen in the previous chapters, our directive does not inherit from its parent scope, but rather uses the isolated scope, meaning it has its own scope:

```
.directive('charts', [function () {

  return {
    restrict: 'EA',
    template: '<div></div>',
    scope: {
      config: '='
    },
    ...
}
```

Three types of local scope properties can be added into the isolated scope: @ (One-way binding), = (Two-way binding), and & (Expressions). So every time you use a scope property and assign an object literal, you are using an isolated scope.

There's more...

You can install any Karma plugin using the following command:

```
npm install karma-<plugin name> --save-dev
```

For example, to use the Mocha framework instead of Jasmine, you can install `karma-mocha` with the previous command.

Testing elements when the scope changes

Another important task is to test the directive when the scope has changed.

Getting ready

We are still using the same code from the previous recipe, we just need to add more assertions.

How to do it...

1. Open the `charts.spec.js` file at `app/modules/shared/directives/charts/` and add the following highlighted code:

    ```
    // Update chart when scope change
      it('should update chart', function() {
        $scope.config.data.columns.pop();
        $scope.$digest();
    ```

```
    expect(iSo.config.data.columns.length).toBe(3);
});

//if no type is specified it should be set to line
it('should have a default line chart type', function() {
    $scope.$digest();
    expect(iSo.config.type).toEqual('line');
});
```

2. Let's run the tests again. Click on the Play button at the top of WebStorm. Now we can see two more tests, one for `update chart` and another for `chart type`, as we can see in the following screenshot:

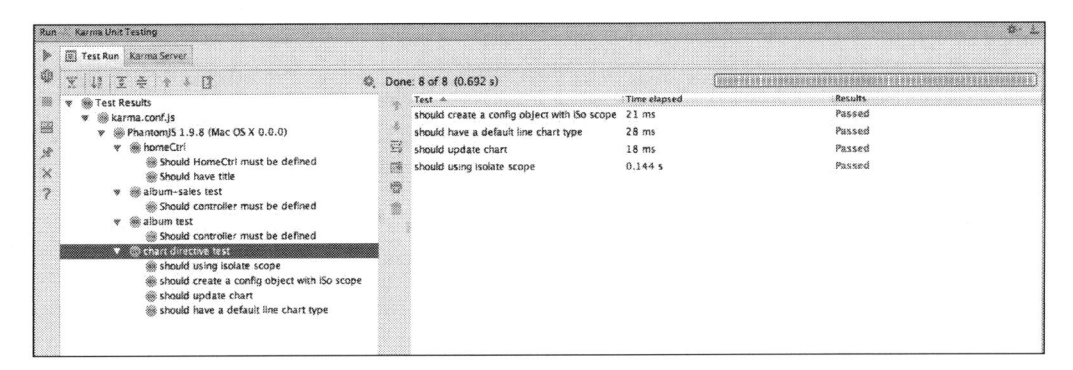

How it works...

Let's see what happens in the previous block of code:

```
it('should update chart', function() {
    $scope.config.data.columns.pop();
    $scope.$digest();
    expect(iSo.config.data.columns.length).toBe(3);
});
```

Using the `$scope.config.data.columns.pop()`, we removed one column from the chart, and used the `$scope.$digest();` to render the chart after the change.

Directive Unit Testing with Karma and Jasmine

The same is done on the second block:

```
it('should have a default line chart type', function() {
  $scope.$digest();
  expect(iSo.config.type).toEqual('line');
});
```

But this time we just checked that the directive has a default chart type, if the chart config doesn't have one.

There's more...

WebStorm also offers us the possibility of exporting the test results to an HTML external file and saving it somewhere in our application:

1. Let's see how we can do that. After the tests have finished, click on the export button on the testing toolbar (the last icon), as shown in the following image:

2. Choose the folder you want to save the file to and check the **Open exported file** checkbox, as shown in the following screenshot:

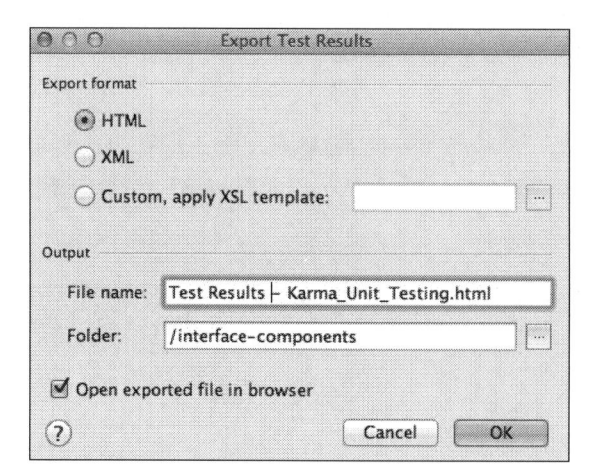

3. The final result from these steps can be found in the following screenshot:

Karma Unit Testing: 8 total, 8 passed — 244 ms

Collapse | Expand

- PhantomJS 1.9.8 (Mac OS X 0.0.0) — 244 ms
  - **homeCtrl** — 24 ms
    - Should HomeCtrl must be defined — passed — 18 ms
    - Should have title — passed — 6 ms
  - **album-sales test** — 5 ms
    - Should controller must be defined — passed — 5 ms
  - **album test** — 4 ms
    - Should controller must be defined — passed — 4 ms
  - **chart directive test** — 211 ms
    - should using isolate scope — passed — 144 ms
    - should create a config object with iSo scope — passed — 21 ms
    - should update chart — passed — 18 ms
    - should have a default line chart type — passed — 28 ms

Index

Symbols

$apply() function 12
$http.get() method 118

A

accordion tabs directives 56-60
Angular Bootstrap UI
  URL 44
AngularJS
  documentation, URL 122
  version 2, URL 126
AngularJS apps
  testing, with Karma 166-173
  testing, with Karma Runner 166-173
angularjs-google-maps
  URL 85
AngularJS project
  scaling 137
  scaling, for using reusable
        directives 138-145
AngularJS UI Bootstrap
  URL 52
AngularJS UI directives
  accordion tabs directives 56
  isolated scope 52
  modal directives 40
  tab directive 46
angular-loading-bar directive
  about 85
  URL 85

B

baseline app
  creating, with generator-angm 78, 79
Bootstrap UI directives
  avoiding, in dealing with tabs 13-22
built-in directives
  ng-hide 1
  ng-repeat 1
  ng-show 1

C

C3.js
  reference manual, URL 157
compile function
  about 125
  using 68-70, 126
compiler
  about 70
  compile phase 70
  link phase 70
  URL 71
content
  mixing, on templates 128-135
Content Delivery Network (CDN) 157
controller function, directive
  about 32, 33
  URL 35
  using 33-35
custom CSS
  about 103
  applying 103-106
custom validation
  used, for creating form directive 157-164

D

D3
  URL 146
data attribute
  about 35
  using, for HTML5 compilation 35-37
Dependency Injection (DI) 13
Directive Definition Object (DDO)
  about 4
  URL 13
directives
  building, as interface component 145-151
  controller function 32
  dynamic templates, using 118-124
  example 64-66
  testing, on scope change 180-183
  test, writing with Jasmine 173-180
  URL 4
Document Object Model (DOM)
  about 1
  manipulating, with jQuery 66-68
Don't Repeat Yourself (DRY) 138
draggable widget
  URL 72
droppable widget
  URL 75
dynamic content
  loading 60-62
dynamic directives
  organizing, on shared folders 126-128
dynamic templates
  dealing with 117
  using, on directives 118-25

E

external templates
  loading, for best practices 7-10

F

files, navbar folder
  navabar-test.js 25
  navbarCtrl.js 25
  navbar.html 25
  navbarRoute.js 25

form directive
  creating, with custom validation 157-164

G

generator
  best practices 80, 81
generator-angm
  URL 78
  used, for creating baseline app 78, 79
Google CDN
  URL 82
grunt dev command
  URL 81
Gruntfile 97

H

HTML5 compilation
  data attribute, using for 35-37

I

inline HTML templates
  about 2
  using 2-4
interface component
  directive, building as 145-157
isolated scope
  about 52-54
  attribute 54
  bindings 54
  expressions 54
  URL 55

J

Jasmine
  used, for writing tests for directives 173-179
jQuery
  used, for manipulating DOM 66-68
jQuery Lite 12, 64
jQuery UI
  draggable directive, creating 71, 72
  droppable directive, creating 73, 74

K

Karma
  testing, with AngularJS apps 166-172
  URL 173
Karma Runner
  testing, with AngularJS apps 166-172

L

LESS
  URL 106
link function
  about 11, 124
  using 11-13, 68-70

M

modal directive
  creating 4-7
modal directives
  dealing with 40-43
  working 44-46

N

navbar directive
  building 24-29
ng-grid directive
  about 88
  implementing 88-93
  static JSON file, URL 91
  URL 93
ngMap directive
  about 82
  implementing 82-84
ngModel
  about 163
  URL 164
ng-style() directive 7
ng-transclude
  URL 7

O

Off Canvas menu
  about 95-102
  URL 95

P

PhantomJS
  URL 173
Polymer
  URL 138
postLink()function 68

R

reusable directives
  used, by scaling AngularJS project 138-145

S

scope.$apply() method 66
shared folders
  dynamic directives, organizing 126-128
shopping cart
  building 106-116

T

tab directive
  about 46
  creating 47-49
  working 49-52
tabs
  dealing, without Bootstrap UI directives 13-22
templates
  different content, mixing 128-135

U

ui.bootstrap modal
  URL 103
user interface 39

W

WebStorm
  about 165
  URL 166

Y

Yeoman
  URL 23

Thank you for buying
AngularJS Directives Cookbook

About Packt Publishing

Packt, pronounced 'packed', published its first book, *Mastering phpMyAdmin for Effective MySQL Management*, in April 2004, and subsequently continued to specialize in publishing highly focused books on specific technologies and solutions.

Our books and publications share the experiences of your fellow IT professionals in adapting and customizing today's systems, applications, and frameworks. Our solution-based books give you the knowledge and power to customize the software and technologies you're using to get the job done. Packt books are more specific and less general than the IT books you have seen in the past. Our unique business model allows us to bring you more focused information, giving you more of what you need to know, and less of what you don't.

Packt is a modern yet unique publishing company that focuses on producing quality, cutting-edge books for communities of developers, administrators, and newbies alike. For more information, please visit our website at www.packtpub.com.

About Packt Open Source

In 2010, Packt launched two new brands, Packt Open Source and Packt Enterprise, in order to continue its focus on specialization. This book is part of the Packt open source brand, home to books published on software built around open source licenses, and offering information to anybody from advanced developers to budding web designers. The Open Source brand also runs Packt's open source Royalty Scheme, by which Packt gives a royalty to each open source project about whose software a book is sold.

Writing for Packt

We welcome all inquiries from people who are interested in authoring. Book proposals should be sent to author@packtpub.com. If your book idea is still at an early stage and you would like to discuss it first before writing a formal book proposal, then please contact us; one of our commissioning editors will get in touch with you.

We're not just looking for published authors; if you have strong technical skills but no writing experience, our experienced editors can help you develop a writing career, or simply get some additional reward for your expertise.

[PACKT] open source
community experience distilled
PUBLISHING

Mastering AngularJS Directives

ISBN: 978-1-78398-158-8   Paperback: 210 pages

Develop, maintain, and test production-ready directives for any AngularJS-based application

1. Explore the options available for creating directives, by reviewing detailed explanations and real-world examples.
2. Dissect the life cycle of a directive and understand why they are the base of the AngularJS framework.
3. Discover how to create structured, maintainable, and testable directives through a step-by-step, hands-on approach to AngularJS.

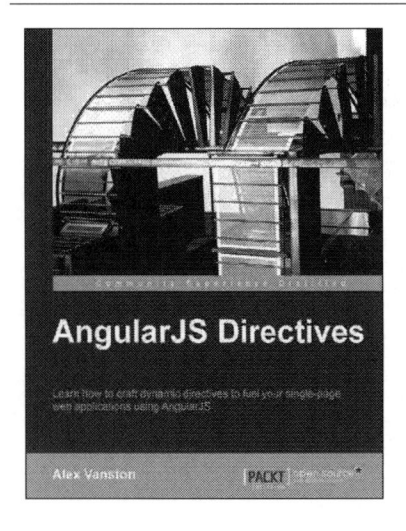

AngularJS Directives

ISBN: 978-1-78328-033-9   Paperback: 110 pages

Learn how to craft dynamic directives to fuel your single page web applications using AngularJS

1. Learn how to build an AngularJS directive.
2. Create extendable modules for plug-and-play usability.
3. Build apps that react in real time to changes in your data model.

Please check www.PacktPub.com for information on our titles

Mastering Web Application Development with AngularJS

ISBN: 978-1-78216-182-0   Paperback: 372 pages

Build single-page web applications using the power of AngularJS

1. Make the most out of AngularJS by understanding the AngularJS philosophy and applying it to real-life development tasks.
2. Effectively structure, write, test, and finally deploy your application.
3. Add security and optimization features to your AngularJS applications.
4. Harness the full power of AngularJS by creating your own directives.

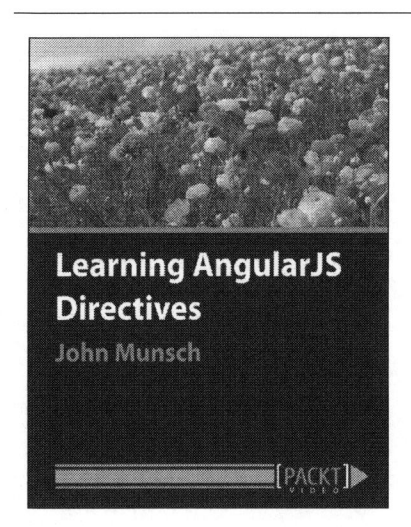

Learning AngularJS Directives (Video)

ISBN: 978-1-78528-732-9   Duration: 01:00 hours

Get to grips with AngularJS directives to create dynamic and responsive web applications quickly and easily

1. Delve into the various concepts behind creating functional and interactive directives.
2. Create your own customized HTML elements by using SVG and HTML5 canvas.
3. Learn about isolate scope and transclusion and put these into action when writing code.

Please check **www.PacktPub.com** for information on our titles

Made in the USA
Middletown, DE
19 December 2016